A Survival Kit for Doctoral Students and Their Supervisors

This book is dedicated to Steinar Kvale.

A Survival Kit for Doctoral Students and Their Supervisors

Traveling the Landscape of Research

Lene Tanggaard
Aalborg University

Charlotte Wegener
Aalborg University

Los Angeles | London | New Delhi
Singapore | Washington DC | Melbourne

FOR INFORMATION:

SAGE Publications, Inc.
2455 Teller Road
Thousand Oaks, California 91320
E-mail: order@sagepub.com

SAGE Publications Ltd.
1 Oliver's Yard
55 City Road
London, EC1Y 1SP
United Kingdom

SAGE Publications India Pvt. Ltd.
B 1/I 1 Mohan Cooperative Industrial Area
Mathura Road, New Delhi 110 044
India

SAGE Publications Asia-Pacific Pte. Ltd.
3 Church Street
#10–04 Samsung Hub
Singapore 049483

Acquisitions Editor: Leah Fargotstein
Editorial Assistant: Yvonne McDuffee
Production Editor: Bennie Clark Allen
Copy Editor: Terri Lee Paulsen
Typesetter: Hurix Systems Pvt. Ltd.
Proofreader: Ellen Brink
Indexer: Mary Mortensen
Cover Designer: Anupama Krishnan
Marketing Manager: Susannah Goldes

Printed in the United States of America

Names: Tanggaard, Lene, author. | Wegener, Charlotte, author.

Title: A survival kit for doctoral students and their supervisors : traveling the landscape of research / Lene Tanggaard, Aalborg University; Charlotte Wegener, Aalborg University.

Description: Los Angeles : SAGE Publications, 2016. | Includes bibliographical references and index.

Identifiers: LCCN 2015040060 | ISBN 9781483379449 (pbk. : alk. paper)

Subjects: LCSH: Doctor of philosophy degree—Handbooks, manuals, etc. | Doctoral students—Handbooks, manuals, etc. | Graduate students—Handbooks, manuals, etc. | Universities and colleges—Graduate work—Handbooks, manuals, etc.

Classification: LCC LB2386. T36 2016 | DDC 378.2—dc23 LC record available at http://lccn.loc .gov/2015040060

This book is printed on acid-free paper.

SFI Certified Sourcing
www.sfiprogram.org
SFI-00453

16 17 18 19 20 10 9 8 7 6 5 4 3 2 1

Brief Contents

Preface   xiii

Acknowledgments   xxv

About the Authors   xxvii

Chapter 1: Theoretical Basis of the Book   1

Chapter 2: Matching Student and Research Community   19

Chapter 3: Originality and Contribution   37

Chapter 4: Making the Most of Obstacles   57

Chapter 5: Peers and Masters Are Everywhere   77

Chapter 6: Doing Supervision   95

Chapter 7: Feedback—Part of Making It Work   115

Chapter 8: "Get a Life" or Simply "Live Your Life"   139

Index   158

Detailed Contents

Preface   xiii

Acknowledgments   xxv

About the Authors   xxvii

Chapter 1: Theoretical Basis of the Book   1

  Abstract   1

  An Apprenticeship Perspective   1

  Why Apprenticeship?   2

    The Researcher as Instrument   3

    Learning Through Other People's Accounts   4

    A Distributed Notion of Apprenticeship   5

  Things Elites Can Teach Us   5

  What Is Apprenticeship in Research, and

    What Can Be Learned From It?   7

  The PhD Endeavor as a Journey   8

    Into the Landscape of Research   8

    A Question of Belonging   9

    Apprenticeship Pedagogy   10

  A Pedagogy of Doing   11

  Moving Away From Pure Learning   13

    Plato   13

    The Dualism of Form and Content   13

    The Dualism of Body and Mind   14

  Good Advice for the PhD Student   15

  Good Advice for the Supervisor   15

  Conclusion   16

  References   16

Chapter 2: Matching Student and Research Community   19

Abstract   19
Successful and Unsuccessful Matching   20
Why Research Talent Is Relationally
    Defined and Achieved   20
Relational Talents   21
Finding the Right Match   22
    Reciprocal Trust   23
    Lene's Story: Is This a Place to Work?   24
What Is Needed to Find the Match?   26
    Svend's Story About Jumping on the Right Train   26
Mismatch   28
    Rasmus's Story About Mismatch   28
    Failing Is Not the End of the World   30
Finishing on Time?   30
    Ninna's Story About Finishing on Time   32
Why Matching Can Be Difficult   33
Good Advice for the PhD Student   34
Good Advice for the Supervisor   34
Conclusion   35
References   35

Chapter 3: Originality and Contribution   37

Abstract   37
Making an Impact   37
    "Forced Novelty"   38
    "We're All Individuals"   39
We Have to Work It Out Ourselves—But How?   40
    Traveling Occupied Territory   40
    Developing Voice   41
    Conventions   42
An Experiment of Disarmament   43
    Writing Dialogues   43
    Defensive Writing   43
    Ninna's Letter   44
    Charlotte's Letter   45
Dismantling Pretentious Scientific Language   46
    Balancing Originality and Convention With Kvale   46
    Dismantling Pretentious Language   47
Complying and Adjustment   48
    Encouraging Creative Thinking   49

"Stretching" and "Habits of the Mind"   49
Questioning the Research Question   50
    Charlotte's Research Question   50
    Changing the Plans   51
    Immersed in the Field   51
    Dialogue Between Data and Theory   52
    A New Research Approach   53
Good Advice for the PhD Student   54
Good Advice for the Supervisor   54
Conclusion   54
References   55

Chapter 4: Making the Most of Obstacles   57

Abstract   57
Research as a Creative Endeavor   57
How Can I Contribute and Do Creative Research?   58
    How to Apply Creative Processes to PhD Work   58
Data on Deviations and Research in Everyday Life   59
    To Stumble and Learn   59
How Can We Stumble Creatively?   60
    Relearning the Joy of Experimentation   61
Absorption and Deadlines   61
    Undisturbed Concentration   62
    Lene's Constant Distractions   62
    Charlotte's Friday Detour   64
    When We Skip   65
Forced Incubation   66
Apprenticeships and Quick Learning   67
    A "Fast-Food" Mentality   67
    Creativity Cannot Be Hurried   68
    Craftsman   69
The McDonaldization of Research   69
    Efficiency   70
    Calculability   71
    Predictability   71
    Control   71
    Quality and Quantity   72
Good Advice for the PhD Student   73
Good Advice for the Supervisor   73
Conclusion   74
References   74

Chapter 5: Peers and Masters Are Everywhere   77

Abstract   77
Distributed Masters   77
Apprenticeship Writing   78
   Fear and Anxiety   78
   Supporting a Peer-Review Culture   79
Writing and Identity Formation in Peer Groups   79
Writing Throughout the Journey   80
Networks   81
Writing Groups   81
   Mutuality, Expertise, and Writer Identity   82
   Scene From a Peer Writing Group   82
   A Neat Literature Review   83
   Sharing Experience and Know-How   83
   Questions of Writer Identity   84
   Including Yourself in the Text   84
   Academic, Social, and Emotional Support   85
Do I Have the Time . . . and the Courage?   85
   Too Time-Consuming   85
   Revealing Writings in Progress   86
   Nonproductive Peer Interaction   86
Life Itself Is a Master   87
   The Memoir of a Nobel Prize Winner   87
   Unscientific Method Chapters?   88
   Use Your Life Experience   89
   Knowledge Brokering   89
   Pragmatic Ideals   90
Be a Master Yourself   90
Good Advice for the PhD Student   91
Good Advice for the Supervisor   91
Conclusion   92
References   92

Chapter 6: Doing Supervision   95

Abstract   95
Supervision as Process and Production   95
Coauthorship as a Pedagogic Practice   96
   E-Mails as Real-Time Data   97
The Coauthor Study   98
   Inviting in—Unconditionally Accepting   99
   Idea Testing and Getting the Student to Work   100

Theoretical Framing   101

Focused Asking for Advice and Making
    Structural Adjustments   102

Fine-Tuning and Some Deletions   104

Sharing Completion   105

Extending the Radius of the Research Community   106

A Pedagogy of Doing   108

The "First-Cut Publisher"   109

Advantages and Pitfalls   110

Sharing and Building of Power   110

Good Advice for the PhD Student   111

Good Advice for the Supervisor   111

Conclusion   112

References   112

Chapter 7: Feedback—Part of Making It Work   **115**

Abstract   115

A Range of Options   116

A Good Writer Is Not Necessarily a Good Writing Teacher   116

Feedback From an Apprenticeship Perspective   117

Klaus' Story About His Supervisor   118

Formative Apprenticeship   119

Thomas Is Told That His Text Has "Potential"   120

Stephen Reflects on Candidate-Dependent
    Supervision   121

Writing for "Real" and "Blind" Reviewers   123

"It's All About Desire"   124

The Necessity of Untidy Texts   125

An Untidy Text or "How a Detour Became a Highway"   126

Precious Feedback From Editors   127

The Circularity of Knowing   130

Vlad's Reading Group   131

Vlad's PhD Seminar   131

"People Think by Acting"   132

Charlotte's First Conference   132

Looking for a Second Supervisor   133

Retrospective Preparation?   134

Learning From Giving Feedback   134

Good Advice for the PhD Student   135

Good Advice for the Supervisor   135

Conclusion   136

References   136

Chapter 8: "Get a Life" or Simply "Live Your Life"   **139**

Abstract   139
Putting an End to Uncertainty?   139
Moving Fast or Learning to Live a Researcher's Life?   140
In Search of a Researcher Identity   141
    The Purpose of Learning   141
    The Total Life   142
    Goal Setting as a Mutual Responsibility   142
    Kundera on Slowness   142
Always in the Middle   143
    Entering the Scene   143
    Progressing Along Trajectories of Participation   144
    Something Keeps on Happening for Jonathan and Ken   144
It Is Good to Be Part of Something   147
There Is Always Work To Do   148
Always Heading Somewhere   149
"Let's Start Before We're Ready"   150
    Abandoning the Rules   151
    Unpleasant Confusion   151
Stepping Stones for a Future Career   152
    The Artist Andreas Golder   152
    "I Do Not Know If I'm an Artist"   153
    The Craft of Finding One's Own Style   154
Good Advice for the PhD Student   155
Good Advice for the Supervisor   155
Conclusion   156
References   156

Index   **158**

Preface

Our collaboration began as a student-supervisor relationship. We had written a book chapter and subsequently a journal article together without any physical meetings. We did meet for supervisory reasons; however, all of our shared text production had evolved over e-mail. This real-time textual evidence from the production process turned out to be valuable data about the integrated activity of supervision and the co-production of text. Charlotte suggested we used our e-mails as data in a new cowritten paper and Lene added the apprentice perspective. We decided to present the analysis at a conference arguing for an apprenticeship perspective on supervision. From this perspective, participating in real work and producing real material is a core activity of the doctoral learning process. Likewise, the supervisor is involved in real production, not just to produce text for publication but as an integral part of the supervisory endeavor.

This book extends the apprenticeship perspective to other areas of doctoral scholarship and supervision. An apprenticeship perspective is not a prescription for good practice, but rather a lens that illuminates practices related to doctoral training; some of these are highly planned and orderly, others messy and odd. In adopting this perspective, the intention is to get closer to the actual and messy practices of doctoral training than many "how-to" books ever come.

The conference presentation was well attended. What especially struck us were audience questions about academic hierarchy and power relations between student and supervisor. "How did you dare to ask your supervisor to cowrite?" one doctoral student asked Charlotte. "If I am ever going to cowrite with my supervisor, *she* must ask *me*," she said. We took these kinds of questions as serious advice. There is much more in this than just an enjoyable experience of cowriting. Traveling the landscape of research is challenging. A survival kit is comforting if you are worried about getting lost in the wilderness. It may even be lifesaving if disaster strikes. The title of the book refers to both purposes. The book aims to reduce worries, thus making us all more courageous, and it contains first-aid equipment useful in hard times. We do not claim any easy shortcuts, nor do we claim cowriting to be particularly troublesome. But we do claim that joy can be a guidepost, which goes hand in hand with academic ambition and achievement.

Our studies presented in the present book show that the research students who succeed in carrying out their doctoral training are good at setting up an extended network of learning resources among peers and colleagues. They test themselves in developing relations and engaging in peer writing, presenting preliminary results at conferences, and challenging themselves through submission of their work to journals. The feedback they get from peers, cowriters, and colleagues contributes to early and tangible input to work in progress.

Supervisors can also benefit more extensively from engaging in the work. Our studies indicate that it is a trap for learning in doctoral training when supervisors cannot figure out how to share their knowledge. Many specialists cannot put into words what they do. They have difficulty verbalizing their knowledge. They are competent practitioners but lack a language for it or perhaps do not have a feeling of how to pass it on. If you are not outgoing as a master and do not invite other people into your practice, you run the risk that your expertise is not transferred to others, and also that your work is not subject to the criticism that can be a prerequisite for further development. You do not get the opportunity to unpack and share your knowledge in an academic community. A skilled organization of the craft, in relation to doctoral training, will therefore promote mentorship and formulate standards that are possible for everyone to understand. It is vital that those responsible are able and have the opportunity to invest resources in training novices.

Throughout the book, we share with the reader a bunch of stories about doctoral training, research perspectives on the practice of learning during the doctoral journey. We have invited our colleagues to co-reflect with us in the form of personal narratives and reflections from their own research journeys. The various scenarios and narratives focus on the personal side of doctoral training and supervision rather than the more technical sides. Our aim is to unpack and share. We believe that learning how to be a researcher is the practice of a craft, very different from following a recipe. The advice we will give throughout the book is based on practice, our own and others, reflecting the kind of learning we believe is fruitful for both doctoral students and supervisors. The aim of the book is to support and inspire both students and supervisors in the humanities and social sciences to make the PhD endeavor a creative and stimulating experience for all involved parties. We advocate an apprenticeship learning perspective to shed light on the dynamics of the student–supervisor interaction, to show the potential for mutual learning and production, and also to reveal the diverse range of learning resources beyond the formal supervisory relationship.

Why is an apprenticeship perspective needed? The simple answer is that we are witness to huge problems related to drop-out and lack of successful learning experiences in doctoral training. A study of doctoral students at 29 U.S. and Canadian universities reports that only 40% to 50% of PhD candidates complete their programs within a decade (e.g., Sowell, Zhang, Bell, & Kirby, 2010). The report concludes that attrition runs high in PhD programs, despite rigorous selection processes in graduate schools and high general academic achievement levels among those seeking doctoral degrees. Attrition is highest in the humanities, while the completion rates are higher in mathematics and the physical sciences. Amundsen and McAlpine (2011) report that attrition rates in the social sciences range from 30% to 50%, depending on the subject area. However, they also advocate a broader institutional and disciplinary contextual perspective on PhD completion, thus paying attention to barriers and facilitators to learning and the development of academic identity.

Studies have found that those who completed their dissertations were able to operate independently but sought the emotional support of others, whereas those who did not complete had difficulty seeking support (McAlpine, Paulson, Gonsalves, & Jazvac-Martek, 2012). The call is for pedagogies that emphasize relational, rather than regulatory practices, as noted by Devenish et al. (2009). Thus, this present book caters to the increasing interest in relationships between learners and the way knowledge is coproduced (Lassig, Dillon, & Diezmann, 2013). The book embraces coproduction in its broadest sense. We would like to express our sincere thanks to our colleagues who devoted their time and knowledge in their writing for this book. Their stories open up to wider landscapes and point to the vastness of possible routes to travel.

Overview of the Chapters

The book is divided into eight chapters. The first introduces the landscape metaphor and argues for an apprenticeship perspective on doctoral learning and supervision. Each of the remaining chapters draws on theory and empirical data to address the theme of the chapter and closes with some inspirational questions and practical exercises that the student and supervisor can take into consideration and try out, individually and together. The book is chronologically structured, starting with the students' initial contact with a research community and a potential supervisor and ending with the completed dissertation, oral defense, and beyond. However, each chapter can be read separately depending on the needs and interests of the reader. The content of the chapters is as follows:

1. Theoretical Basis of the Book

This chapter introduces situated notions of research practice as "doing" and "knowing," involving different parties, activities, goals, and circumstances in landscapes of research (Nielsen, 2008; Nielsen & Tanggaard, 2011). Human doing and knowing are flexible engagements with the world entailing "open-ended processes of improvisation with the social, material, and experiential resources at hand" (Lave, 1993/2009, p. 204). Lave argues that there are no fixed boundaries between an activity and its settings; between cognitive, bodily, and social forms of activity; and between problems and solutions (Lave, 1988). Her practice theory aims at the integration of emotion, motivation, and agency, and pays particular attention to "differences among participants, and to the on-going struggles that develop across activities around those differences" (Holland & Lave, 2009, p. 5).

The chapter describes how learning contexts—traditionally conceived as bounded containers—have been reconceptualized by situated learning (Lave & Wenger, 1991) as more fluid and relational (Edwards, Biesta, & Thorpe, 2009). In this light, the "landscape" is introduced as a metaphor running through the chapters. Becher and Trowler (2001, p. 16) note that "land exists without an observer, but landscape does not: the 'scape' is the projection of human consciousness, the way the land is perceived and responded to." Engeström (2009, p. 312) describes the research landscape "as a terrain of activity to be dwelled in and explored." The terrain has existing trails, as well as landmarks and boundaries made by others, and when new dwellers enter the terrain, they "both adapt to the dominant trails and struggle to break away from them" (Engeström, 2009, p. 313). In this conceptual context, the nature of the doctoral student's agency is regarded as the increased capability to traverse the terrain effectively and independently.

2. Matching Student and Research Community

Viewed from the perspective of a landscape metaphor, it becomes evident that not all landscapes are suitable for everybody. Some landscapes will be more congenial or inhabitable than others, and in this chapter we identify criteria that potential PhD students might apply when commencing their doctoral work and trying to find an appropriate research landscape. Ideally, one should seek the perfect fit between the needs and requirements within the research landscape (the kind of research activities, profiles, and new projects) and the qualifications, competences, and interests of the student. However, such an ideal fit is rare. This chapter addresses some of the guiding criteria students might apply when choosing a research career, and it also considers what the supervisor might want to look for when making space for and employing a student. Criteria for the student to look for relate to research publications (what kinds and why), research activities, number of seminars, number of former and current PhD students, grants received, stories from former students, and general public recognition of the research group. For the supervisor, it might be relevant to carefully inquire into the motivation, writing skills, ambitions, level of former engagement in other research landscapes, relevance of the proposal, and originality of ideas. It is imperative for potential researchers to find a place that conducts research that really suits them. After doing their research and reading published papers, they must actually go there, talk to people, and make sure there is a genuine research environment. For both parties, the key question is how one can explore the destination before beginning the journey, while still being open to surprises and taking risks.

3. Originality and Contribution

This chapter addresses the phase in which the student must design a research project and formulate initial research questions. This work is open-ended and always subject to revision, as research questions often evolve throughout the study. For the supervisor, this involves a delicate balance between guidance and trust.

An essential point of the chapter is that research questions have an evolutionary character. First, iterations of questions are tentative and exploratory, and these broader research questions are sometimes not stated as questions but rather as study objectives. Sub-questions narrow the focus and, while allowing for discovery, they also give direction to the particular kinds of data to collect. Thus, questions become "tools for discovery as well as tools for clarity and focus" (Agee, 2009, p. 446). Based on Alvesson and Sandberg (2013), we argue that "gap-spotting" seems to be the dominant strategy for designing most studies in management, sociology, psychology, and education. However, such gap-spotting rarely produces new and interesting theories, because it neither challenges basic assumptions that underlie existing theories nor those which underlie one's own assumptions. The chapter addresses the fact that research questions usually originate with the researchers' personal biographies and their social contexts (Flick, 2009). Similarly, Agee (2009) finds that many of her students are "in love" with a particular theory even before shaping their questions and that their own life experiences have often played a role in their choices of research topics. This chapter suggest strategies for making use of the energy and commitment inherent in personal experiences and preoccupations. On the other hand, we also discuss how the student's personal theories can be questioned, expanded, and modified through different assumption-challenging approaches.

4. Making the Most of Obstacles

This chapter addresses how to create a productive and rewarding life as a researcher by making the most of obstacles and treating them as challenges. Similar to the other chapters, we view this theme in a situated perspective, acknowledging that researchers are co-constructers of their own learning opportunities. Thus, robustness to and creative ways of handling problems are not tied to the individual but depend extensively on social and distributed forces. We propose ways to find and invite peers and seek out learning opportunities within the immediate environment of the local research group, as well as in other communities nationally and internationally. We also discuss resources for inspiration outside academia and recommend ways in which family life, hobbies, whims, and coincidences can serve as inspiration and thus enhance motivation. We even suggest ways in which procrastination can be productive.

5. Peers and Masters Are Everywhere

In an academic environment, learning is often an individual rather than a group undertaking and student isolation is a frequent problem (Nordentoft, Thomsen, & Wichmann-Hansen, 2012). There are, however, increasing calls for knowledge creation to be collaborative, and writing groups are increasingly subject to empirical studies and theorizing (Maher et al., 2008; Maher, Fallucca, & Mulhern Halasz, 2013). Jazvac-Martek, Chen, and McAlpine (2011) suggest that academic futures of doctoral students depend on their ability to develop and maintain a network of relationships. Similarly, Boud and Lee (2005) challenge a vertical view on individual supervision relationships as the privileged site of pedagogy and suggest a horizontal and distributed view based on the notion of peer learning, theorized and situated within a notion of communities of research practice.

Some studies argue that the doctoral advisor may be the single most critical person for students during the doctoral process (Barnes & Austin, 2009), while other studies point to the fact that students develop and use networks of personal and academic relationships as sources of support (McAlpine et al., 2012). In the case of supervision, apprenticeship teaching is often practiced in the form of one-to-one interactions between supervisor and student (Walker et al., 2008). Golde and Walker (2006) argue that doctoral education programs should be structured to prepare students to generate new knowledge and critically conserve valuable ideas but also transform such new understanding through writing, teaching, application and publication. In this chapter, we argue that students cannot achieve all of this with the supervisor as the only source of inspiration. Thus, the main point of the chapter is that doctoral processes must include interaction with a diverse range of people and with as many collaborators as possible or as needed by the student.

Work with early-career academics demonstrates a significant impact of group pedagogies on developing effective publication strategies, as well as "the making and remaking of academic identities" (Lee & Boud, 2003, p. 189). The supervisor can act as a facilitator and encourage the students to seek out peers and build a network. However, the student must invest time and energy developing close connections with peers, in order to share work, seek help and feedback, and discuss difficulties and emotions of various kinds (Hopwood, 2010). In this chapter, we consider and propose ways to do this and outline several benefits based on our empirical data on peer interactions and processes of becoming writers (Wegener, Meier, & Ingerslev, 2014).

6. Doing Supervision

A report from an interview study on doctoral student writing notes that "regardless of publication success or failure, the whole process was one of tremendous effort and struggle" (Kamler, 2008, p. 290). Similarly, Lee and Boud (2003) identified scholarly writing as "a key site for the generation of fear and anxiety, as well as desire." Kamler (2008) argues that coauthorship with supervisors is a significant pedagogic practice that can enhance the robustness and know-how of emerging scholars, as well as their publication output. There is a need, however, to rethink coauthorship more explicitly as a pedagogic practice, particularly in the humanities and social sciences. In this chapter, we outline ways in which cowriting can yield a steep learning curve for the student, enhance the effectiveness of time spent on supervision, and produce high-quality research articles. While reflections, agreements, and advice during supervision and teaching are not necessarily remembered, transferred, or even understood by the student, a cowriting process continuously produces evidence of the student's experimentation with the material, and with struggling but nonetheless progressing. Learning the craft of writing manifests itself step by step in each version of a manuscript. Thus, the supervisor receives instant feedback about the student's learning, which is difficult to achieve from oral dialogue alone. Likewise, the student receives instant feedback from the supervisor's revisions and additions to the text and experiences the evolution of a tangible product of the learning process.

In other words, what is required to write and get published is not always elicited verbally, detached from the actual everyday process of writing and trying to publish. It lies in the activity itself and is sometimes seen more clearly and precisely by both supervisor and student when they engage in the activity together. Additionally, there is an interest from both parties in getting the work done, as both are dependent on publishing their work. In this light, cowriting must be seen as a mutual investment and, accordingly, yielding mutual benefits. Students serve as "data-providers" and "publishing motors," and students who really learn the craft contribute to more publications, both during the doctoral journey and over the longer term. This shared understanding creates a common purpose, which enables the supervisor to be quite explicit about production expectations and secures the student a fair amount of the supervisor's time and attention. The student gets the opportunity to decode academic writing conventions while reading the supervisory contribution, and at the same time, she is on her own to practice and thus become a critical, creative researcher. Coauthorship helps the students avoid many of the struggles and anxieties of publishing frequently reported as reasons for giving up doctoral studies (Kamler, 2008). Part of this chapter is based on an earlier published article (Wegener & Tanggaard, 2013). We would like to thank the journal *Forum Qualitative Sozialforschung/Forum: Qualitative Social Research* for the permission to use the article in the present context.

7. Feedback—Part of Making It Work

In this chapter, we devote our attention exclusively to feedback and the craft of asking for, benefitting from, and giving feedback. Supervisory feedback is essential for the student's progress and for the completion of a dissertation. Besides this, there is a range of options for dialogue and means of obtaining others' reactions to your work. Feedback can be the product of collaboration and discussions with a colleague, of lecturing, or of presenting a paper at a conference. In a recent review of workplace learning studies, Noe, Clark, and Klein (2014, p. 258) say that access to feedback enhances self-awareness, increases the individual's confidence regarding performance and success, and helps alleviate the stress associated with challenging work experiences. Various examples of access to feedback and the processes of writing with and learning from feedback will be discussed. How, where, and to what end should doctoral students seek out the feedback they need at specific times? How should they deal with serious criticism and make the feedback a source for moving forward?

8. "Get a Life" or Simply "Live Your Life"

You already have a life—and even a good one because you are reading this book! However, postdoctoral life starts long before the dissertation is complete. This chapter suggests several steps for the student during the doctoral process, aiming at building the desired career. Many of these activities also serve as energizers during periods of isolation, disillusion, or writer's block. The chapter describes how to build an idea bank of themes for future papers, how to network when one does not have much time, and ways to become involved in public discussions and activities. As a supervisor, planning for the future includes considerations on how—and whether—to keep the student within the research community, how to give advice about other career possibilities, coauthorship beyond the oral defense, and ways of inviting the student into (wider) research communities.

References

Agee, J. (2009). Developing qualitative research questions: A reflective process. *International Journal of Qualitative Studies in Education, 22*(4), 431–447.

Alvesson, M., & Sandberg, J. (2013). *Constructing research questions: Doing interesting research.* London: Sage.

Amundsen, C., & McAlpine, L. (2011). Moving from evidence to action. In C. Amundsen and L. McAlpine (Eds.), *Doctoral education: Research-based strategies for doctoral students, supervisors and administrators* (pp. 203–211). Netherlands: Springer.

Barnes, B. J., & Austin, A. E. (2009). The role of doctoral advisors: A look at advising from the advisor's perspective. *Innovative Higher Education, 33*(5), 297–315.

Becher, T., & Trowler, P. R. (2001). *Academic tribes and territories: Intellectual enquiry and the culture of disciplines.* Buckingham, UK: Open University Press Milton Keynes.

Boud, D., & Lee, A. (2005). "Peer learning" as pedagogic discourse for research education. *Studies in Higher Education, 30*(5), 501–516.

Devenish, R., Dyer, S., Jefferson, T., Lord, L., van Leeuwen, S., & Fazakerley, V. (2009). Peer to peer support: The disappearing work in the doctoral student experience. *Higher Education Research & Development, 28*(1), 59–70.

Edwards, R., Biesta, G., & Thorpe, M. (2009). *Rethinking contexts for learning and teaching: Communities, activities and networks*. London & New York: Taylor & Francis.

Engeström, Y. (2009). The future of activity theory: A rough draft. In A. Sannino, H. Daniels, and K. D. Gutiérrez (Eds.), *Learning and expanding with activity theory* (303–328). Cambridge: Cambridge University Press.

Flick, U. (2009). *An introduction to qualitative research*. Thousand Oaks, CA: Sage.

Golde, C. M., & Walker, G. E. (2006). *Envisioning the future of doctoral education: Preparing stewards of the discipline*. San Francisco, CA: Carnegie Essays on the Doctorate, Jossey-Bass–Carnegie Foundation for the Advancement of Teaching.

Holland, D., & Lave, J. (2009). Social practice theory and the historical production of persons. *Actio: An International Journal of Human Activity Theory, 2*(1), 1–15.

Hopwood, N. (2010). A sociocultural view of doctoral students' relationships and agency. *Studies in Continuing Education, 32*(2), 103–117.

Jazvac-Martek, M., Chen, S., & McAlpine, L. (2011). Tracking the doctoral student experience over time: Cultivating agency in diverse spaces. In L. McAlpine and C. Amundsen (Eds.), *Doctoral education: Research-based strategies for doctoral students, supervisors and administrators* (17–36). London: Springer.

Kamler, B. (2008). Rethinking doctoral publication practices: Writing from and beyond the thesis. *Studies in Higher Education, 33*(3), 283–294.

Lassig, C. J., Dillon, L. H., & Diezmann, C. M. (2013). Student or scholar? Transforming identities through a research writing group. *Studies in Continuing Education, 35*(3), 299–314.

Lave, J. (1988). *Cognition in practice: Mind, mathematics and culture in everyday life*. Cambridge: University Press.

Lave, J. (1993/2009). The practice of learning. In K. Illeris (Ed.), *Contemporary theories of learning: Learning theorists in their own words* (200–208). London and New York: Routledge.

Lave, J., & Wenger, E. (1991). *Situated learning: Legitimate peripheral participation*. Cambridge: Cambridge University Press.

Lee, A., & Boud, D. (2003). Writing groups, change and academic identity: Research development as local practice. *Studies in Higher Education, 28*(2), 187–200.

Maher, D., Seaton, L., McMullen, C., Fitzgerald, T., Otsuji, E, & Lee, A. (2008). "Becoming and being writers": The experiences of doctoral students in writing groups. *Studies in Continuing Education, 30*(3), 263–275.

Maher, M., Fallucca, A., & Mulhern Halasz, H. (2013). Write on! through to the Ph.D.: Using writing groups to facilitate doctoral degree progress. *Studies in Continuing Education, 35*(2), 193–208.

McAlpine, L., Paulson, J., Gonsalves, A., & Jazvac-Martek, M. (2012). "Untold" doctoral stories: Can we move beyond cultural narratives of neglect? *Higher Education Research & Development, 31*(4), 511–523.

Nielsen, K. (2008). The Learning landscape of art and craft. In K. Nielsen, S. Brinkmann, C. Elmholdt et al. (Eds.), *A qualitative stance: Essays in honor of Steinar Kvale*. Aarhus: Aarhus Universitetsforlag.

Nielsen, K., & Tanggaard, L. (2011). Apprenticeship rehabilitated in a postmodern world? *Journal of Vocational Education & Training, 63*(4), 563–573.

Noe, R. A., Clarke, A. D. M. & Klein, H. J. (2014). Learning in the Twenty-First Century Workplace. *Annual Review of Organizational Psychology and Organ. Behavior,* 1: 245–275.

Nordentoft, H. M., Thomsen, R., & Wichmann-Hansen, G. (2012). Collective academic supervision: A model for participation and learning in higher education. *Higher Education, 65*(5), 581–593.

Sowell, R. S., Zhang T., Bell, N. E., & Kirby, S. N. (2010). *PhD completion and attrition: Policies and practices to promote student success.* Washington, DC: Council of Graduate Schools.

Walker, G. E., Golde, C. M., Jones, L., et al. (2008). *The formation of scholars: Rethinking doctoral education for the twenty-first century.* San Francisco, CA: Jossey-Bass.

Wegener, C., Meier, N., & Ingerslev, K. (2014). Borrowing brainpower—sharing insecurities. Lessons learned from a doctoral peer writing group. *Studies in Higher Education,* ahead-of-print, 1–14.

Wegener, C., & Tanggaard, L. (2013). Supervisor and student co-writing: An apprenticeship perspective. *Forum Qualitative Sozialforschung/Forum: Qualitative Social Research, 14*(3).

Acknowledgments

This book did not come about without the help from many people and institutions. First of all, a big thank you to SAGE Publications and to our editor, Vicki Knight, for being very helpful and generous throughout the project. We are very grateful to be able to publish our book with SAGE, and we hope the final result lives up to some of the expectations. If not, the fault is on our shoulders. Furthermore, the book would not have been published without the help and feedback received from thoughtful reviewers suggesting ways of improving the manuscript.

When preparing the book, we contacted numerous colleagues: Svend Brinkmann, Klaus Nielsen, Thomas Szulevicz, Stephen Billett, Rasmus Birk, Vlad Glăveanu, Ninna Meier, Jonathan Wyatt, and Ken Gale. We invited them to co-reflect with us through personal narratives from their own research journeys. The personal accounts (our own and others) are meant as reflections on solved and unsolved problems, awkward moments, and lessons learned during doctoral training and supervision—not as general recipes to be followed. As such, we are grateful they have allowed us to use their stories in the book.

We would also like to express our thanks to our daily workplace, Aalborg University in Denmark. We cannot think of any other university being so encouraging of its academic personnel, trusting its employees in all aspects of academic life, and allowing us time to write this book. Furthermore, we would like to thank the Danish Business Research Committee (Erhvervsforskerudvalget) and The Research and Innovation Council in Denmark (Forsknings-og Innovationsstyrelsen) for supporting Charlotte's PhD project, making our initial collaboration possible.

The purpose of the book is to present an empirically based extended perspective on doctoral scholarship, moving beyond a dual perspective (in which the supervisor is seen as the only resource for learning) and investigating broader resources in the landscape of research training along the lines suggested by Professor Steinar Kvale from Aarhus University. Accordingly, learning how to be a researcher is considered to be the practice of a craft, seeking out various sources of learning, and is very different from following a recipe. Steinar, this book is dedicated to you. Even if you are not among us anymore, we believe you would be the first to critique us for having forgotten so many things. Trust us, we are still working on improving it and we hope our readers will join us in the effort.

Lene Tanggaard
Department of Communication and Psychology
Aalborg University
Kroghstræde 3, 9220 Aalborg, Denmark
E-mail: lenet@hum.aau.dk

Charlotte Wegener
Department of Communication and Psychology
Aalborg University
Kroghstræde 3, 9220 Aalborg, Denmark
E-mail: cw@hum.aau.dk

About the Authors

Lene Tanggaard is professor of psychology in the Department of Communication and Psychology at the University of Aalborg, Denmark, where she serves as director of the QS-research group (30 members, VIP); advisor for several PhD students; codirector of The International Centre for the Cultural Psychology of Creativity (ICCPC); and codirector of the Center for Qualitative Studies, a network of more than 90 professors and researchers concerned with methodology and the development of new research tools (http://www.cqs.aau.dk/). She is regional editor of *The International Journal of Qualitative Research in Education* and coeditor of two other research journals (*Qualitative Studies* and *Nordiske Udkast*) and member of the editorial board at *Nordic Psychology* and *Coaching Psychology*. Recent publications include the book *Fooling Around: Creative Learning Pathways* and the chapter "The Socio-Materiality of Creativity: A Case Study of the Creative Processes in Design Work" (in the volume *Rethinking Creativity: Contributions from Social and Cultural Psychology,* edited by V. P. Glăveanu, A. Gillespie, and J. Valsiner).

Charlotte Wegener is assistant professor of innovation in the Department of Communication and Psychology at the University of Aalborg, Denmark. Her work concerns welfare innovation with a specific focus on education, workplace learning, and research methodology. She teaches writing classes for undergraduate and graduate students and is passionate about making academic writing creative and rewarding. Recent publications include "'Would You Like a Cup of Coffee?' Using the Researcher's Insider and Outsider Positions as a Sensitising Concept" (*Ethnography and Education*), "Writing with Phineas: How a Fictional Character From A. S. Byatt

Helped Me Turn My Ethnographic Data Into a Research Text" (*Cultural Studies—Critical Methodologies*), and "Borrowing Brainpower—Sharing Insecurities: Lessons Learned From a Doctoral Peer Writing Group" (*Studies in Higher Education,* with N. Meier and K. Ingerslev).

Chapter One

Theoretical Basis of the Book

Abstract

Purpose: The purpose of the present chapter is to lay the theoretical foundation for the apprenticeship perspective on doctoral training.

Central message: An apprenticeship perspective on learning in academia sheds light on the potential for mutual learning and production, and also reveals the diverse range of learning resources beyond the formal novice–expert relationship.

Takeaways: Although apprenticeship is a well-known concept in educational research, in this case apprenticeship offers an innovative perspective on future practice and research in academia, allowing more students access to high-quality research training and giving supervisors a chance to combine their own research with their supervision obligations.

Keywords: Apprenticeship, landscapes of research, craft, embodied and materialized practices, epistemologies of the hand, distributed notions of apprenticeship, research cultures, apprenticeship pedagogies, impure learning.

An Apprenticeship Perspective

An apprenticeship perspective on doctoral training and supervision involves an emphasis on research as a result of yearlong practice and involvement in research environments, and it is in some sense an antidote to a notion

1

of research talent and research output as a matter of individual talent and ex nihilo originality. Instead, as a term, apprenticeship underlines continuity across generations, traditions, collaboration, and craft. It entails an understanding that "learning, knowledgeability, skilfulness, whatever else they might be, are always only part of ongoing social arrangements and relations" (Lave, 2011, p. 3). This chapter introduces situated notions of research practice as "doing" and "knowing" involving different parties, activities, goals, and circumstances across a "multitude of interrelated events" (Lave, 1993/2009, p. 204) in landscapes of research apprenticeship (Nielsen, 2008; Nielsen et al., 2011). The concepts of landscapes of research and apprenticeship are central in this concern, and they will be unfolded in the following along with references to recent studies on doctoral training and examples taken from various practices of doctoral training and supervision. We will argue why we see apprenticeship as a relevant metaphor and also a very concrete and fruitful practice in doctoral education, and we will discuss the possible limits hereof and the potential barriers in doctoral training seen from this perspective. Our point with this is not to dismiss doctoral training undertaken in school, as when students attend formal PhD courses and get one-to-one supervision, but throughout the book we will embrace a much broader perspective on doctoral education and training and we therefore also need a broader perspective on learning. A view on learning as reduced to formal doctoral education is not enough in this sense. This is why we will also concentrate in this chapter on the notion of practice learning.

Why Apprenticeship?

In a search to describe the qualities of good research training, Kvale (1999) has suggested that research is a craft that can be learned through apprenticeship. Many researchers would probably agree with this. In a recent course on doctoral training in a faculty of medicine in Denmark, where we taught doctors how to incorporate notions of apprenticeship in a training system becoming increasingly more school-oriented, most experienced physicians stated that this is how it is. Or rather, they noted that this is how it ought to be. When asked to elaborate, they were unable to clearly describe the characteristics of the apprenticeship they were referring to. What did they do as supervisors and why? They said only that they had themselves gone through training in laboratories with their advisors and were now trying to do the same with their students. And it is not unusual to have a lack of words when trying to address apprenticeship in research training.

At the center of apprenticeship is the concept that more experienced people assist less experienced ones, providing structure and examples to support the attainment of goals. In the last 20 years, many educators have turned to the concept to get inspiration in designing and supporting learning environments, and concepts such as mentoring, scaffolding, coaching, and cognitive apprenticeship have gained momentum (Dennen, 2004). A cognitive apprenticeship is much like a trade apprenticeship, with learning that occurs as experts and novices interact socially while focused on completing a task. Collins, Brown, and Newman (1989, p. 456) succinctly define it as "learning-through-guided-experience on cognitive and metacognitive, rather than physical, skills and processes." Central parts of this involve modelling, explanations, coaching, scaffolding, reflection, and articulation, whereby the apprentice is guided through the process. However, in this context we will move the concept in a more situated direction underlining not just the cognitive parts of apprenticeship but how apprenticeship is a method or a kind of learning arrangement that makes it easier for doctoral students to get a sense of what research implies and involves and how they can themselves become more experienced researchers.

The Researcher as Instrument

In an interview about research training between Steinar Kvale (the interviewer) and Jean Lave (the interviewee, coauthor of the book *Situated Learning* from 1991, which has served as a paradigmatic book for the whole notion of apprenticeship and situated learning), discussing the importance of methods in research, Lave stated something very similar. When asked if she was guided by a method in her own studies of learning as social practice, Lave noted that she did not carry a method of research in her ethnographic work (Lave & Kvale, 1995). She was unable to describe what she had done through reference to a method, which is often described as a kind of recognized way toward a certain goal. In contrast, she stated that it is the humanity of the researcher that makes her the only instrument sophisticated enough to grasp human life. Summarized here, Lave's message basically was this: I do not carry a method. What I do is based on my existence and on being there. This reluctance to or inability to describe for others the actual practices behind research or research training are maybe a condition, which allows it to happen. If we think too much while doing, we risk being unable to do anything. The idea of the research process as highly situated and flexible is also pointed to from a sociological perspective by Mills (1952/1980, p. 8), who advocates good craftsmanship in which "the fetishism of method and technique" should be avoided. Thus we should all be our own methodologist and theorist, he states.

Apprenticeship learning entails embodied and materialized practices involving both academia and everyday life. This does not only apply to academic research; rather it is a human ability to explore, try out, and practice over and over in dialogue with the world. It is therefore also with a deeply felt respect for practice that this book is written. We know that many aspects of the practices related to doctoral training are more or less inexplicable. However, the book can be read as one long attempt to get a glimpse of these practices in order to get to know them better and also to make the prospective or already-enrolled doctoral student confident with these—not least the newcomer doctoral students who may find many practices odd and incomprehensible. Sometimes just knowing that this is very common can be a big help.

Learning Through Other People's Accounts

Our emphasis on practice and learning by doing has also served as the background for inviting our colleagues to co-reflect with us throughout the book in the form of personal narratives and reflections from their own research journeys. The personal accounts (our own and others) are meant as reflections over unsolved problems, awkward moments, and lessons learned, not as general recipes to be followed. They are necessarily personal statements. As stated by Mills (1952/1980), learning how to be a researcher is the practice of a craft. We are here inspired by Mill's concept of sociological imagination, by which researchers can "understand what is going on in the world and understand what is happening within themselves in their capacity as tiny points of intersection between biography and history in society" (Brinkmann, 2012, p. 18). The researcher's biography and thus the researcher's experience, theoretical orientation, and expectations are important aspects of the research process. However, the researcher's biography and biographic data are not interesting in themselves. In order to achieve novel insights of high quality, introspective, auto-ethnographic accounts must serve only as starting points for thematic, reflective inquiry as Delamont (2009) reminds us. We are convinced, though, that one account is more valuable than "a dozen codifications of procedure by specialists," as Mills (1952/1980, p. 63) puts it:

> Only by conversations in which experienced thinkers exchange information about their actual ways of working can a useful sense of method and theory be imparted to the beginning student.

Likewise, in a paper titled "Towards an Epistemology of the Hand," Brinkmann and Tanggaard (2010) argue, in line with this pragmatic perspective, that experiencing the world—and knowing it—are functions of our practical activities, of our *handling* the world and its problematic situations. What we experience and know about the world are primarily aspects of things that we interact with and manipulate (literally "operate with our hands"). We do not always see clearly beforehand why we do certain things. Things are not first and foremost entities independent of organisms that have objective physical characteristics that can be *seen*. Rather, "things are objects to be treated, used, acted upon and with, enjoyed and endured, even more than things to be known. They are things *had* before they are things cognized" (Dewey, 1925, p. 21). This book is therefore not to be read as a prescription for good practice, but rather as an attempt to illuminate practices related to doctoral training, some of these highly planned and orderly, others messy and odd. In doing so, the intention is to get closer to the actual and messy practices of doctoral training than many "how-to" books ever come. In their review of doctoral advice books as a genre, Kamler and Thomson (2008) found that they frequently produce and reproduce expert–novice power relations that are too often the norm in many universities.

A Distributed Notion of Apprenticeship

We seek to reduce the possibly counterproductive effects of these power relations and address expert–novice relationships in the broadest sense. We engage in reflections with each other, with invited colleagues, and with the literature and thus stress a distributed notion of apprenticeship that opens the door to a wide landscape of resources available for both students and supervisors. Master–student relationships are potentially everywhere. What we must do is seek them out, try them out, and craft them in creative ways. Thus, what we are offering is not just a survival kit but also a kit for adapting or keeping an adventurous mindset. We invite a joint exploration of the social and institutional landscape not only by telling how to do it but also by showing how it happened (Cerwonka & Malkki, 2008, p. 186); what may be typical for students, for their supervisors, for their relationship, what kinds of values, norms, and practices guide doctoral training; and what can be done to make things a little easier, constructive, productive, and helpful for the involved parties. Following this, one natural question does arise: So what does make research education and training easier and more productive?

Things Elites Can Teach Us

In her widely recognized book *Scientific Elite*, written in 1997, Harriet Zuckerman studies from the perspective of sociology the coming into being of recognized Nobel laureates. One of the basic conclusions is that apprenticeship plays a large role in the process of becoming an elite scientist and that being enrolled in apprenticeships with masters already possessing a Nobel Prize enhances the chances and the speed of getting one oneself (Zuckerman, 1997, p. 113). As Zuckerman concludes, the benefits of apprenticeship are a wider orientation in the work of the scientists that includes values and standards of work, norms and attitudes, as well as skills and knowledge. This being the case, apprenticeship in research training involves not only training but also being inducted into a culture (Zuckerman, 1997, p. 123). A chemist explains how she learned a lot from her teacher:

> It's the contact, seeing how they operate, how they think, how they go about things. [Not the specific knowledge?] Not at all. It's learning a style of thinking. I guess. Certainly not the specific knowledge, at least not in the case of Lawrence. There were always people around him who knew more than he did. It wasn't that. It was a method of work that really got things done. (Zuckerman, 1997, p. 122)

And a physicist in the same study sums up the difference between learning the techniques of science and learning to think distinctively as a scientist:

> I knew the techniques of research. I knew a lot of physics. I had the words, the libretto, but not quite the music. In other words, I had not been in contact with men who were deeply imbedded in the traditions of physics: men of high quality. This was my first real contact with first-rate creative minds at the high point of their power. (Zuckerman, 1997, p. 123)

The above quotes highlight how doctoral training requires rather more than the mastery of techniques, as it is dependent on immersion in a given field with the teacher (or master) being a role model for his or her students. The students of chemistry and physics in the above allow themselves to be influenced by how teachers relate to them and by their teachers' attitudes and working methods. Maybe this is even more influential than the other things they learn: the subject matter, skills, and methods. The values and the moral attitude in science and research are often learned through apprenticeship, and it involves much more than just crafts or technique as it includes getting a sense of what kinds of problems you will be able to solve and how. However, apprenticeship is not always harmonious. The study of scientific elites carried out by Zuckerman also evidences examples of conflicts in apprenticeship as when a master is too conservative to recognize new things and does not see the opportunities involved. Moreover, the expectations of master toward apprentice or vice versa may not be transparent and clear to both, which can result in conflicts. The timing of an apprenticeship is also vital as masters can play a large role at specific moments in the process and career of the student while being outplayed or less important at other moments.

What Is Apprenticeship in Research, and What Can Be Learned From It?

The notion of apprenticeship in academia builds upon a perception of research as grounded in activities that are associated with established knowledge and intuitive expertise, which does not necessarily follow analytical and conscious rules. When used in research contexts, it refers to an idea of research as a craft to be practiced and accordingly, from a pragmatic and very practical perspective, the implications hereof are that the doctoral learning process should include "real" activities such as teaching, conference participation, peer review, text production, and publication. However, apprenticeship is more than just getting involved in the activities to develop the skills necessary to become researchers. It is also a matter of identity or constitution of subjectivities, if you like. Becoming a researcher involves taking in, negotiating, and transforming the values, norms, and practices associated with research, making them part of one-self—literally learning how to participate in a constantly changing social practice, gradually developing an identity as someone being a member of the community (Lave & Wenger, 1991). In this sense, identity is "the meeting point," the point of suture between the discourses and practices that makes us part of social practices and simultaneously makes us into subjects who can take in the discourses of the research landscape and use them as researchers.

Unfortunately, many students do not encounter positive apprenticeship experiences and may therefore fail to develop their full potential, involving adequate skills, a sense of belonging, and an identity as a researcher (Walker, Golde, Jones, Bueschel, & Hutchins, 2008). Everyone involved in doctoral education knows that "doctoral work is associated with a number of anxieties" (Kamler & Thomson, 2006, p. 1). Some of these result from misguided assumptions, for example the idea that writing is something you do after you have collected the data or produced the empirical material. However, if research in itself is seen as writing, then the anxieties and the struggles related to writing may be minimized, and writing can become a social practice integral to the everyday life of the student, not an incomprehensible "big thing" or a burden to accomplish at the end of the research journey (Kamler & Thomson, 2008). Our book aims to inspire students and supervisors through revealing how the diverse anxieties related to the whole doctoral training process can be dealt with or even avoided.

The PhD Endeavor as a Journey

What does it mean in both a theoretical and a practical sense to view doctoral training as a journey in the apprenticeship landscape of doctoral research? In the following sections, we will describe the basic principles and aspects related to this view. These are based around the notions of a research landscape, research as a social practice, participation and identity, structural resources, access to research, and transparency of norms and values. In more practical terms this involves a very hands-on grip as to what it means to be a doctoral student, underlining this as being about much more than just individual readiness and skills accumulation. Let's develop this point a bit further.

Into the Landscape of Research

Nielsen and Tanggaard (2011) explain that the style of learning implied in the apprenticeship perspective, without being exclusively tied with this, underlines the importance of access to and transparency in the field of learning. Accordingly, this book addresses the PhD endeavor as a journey into the landscape of research—a journey that is highly dependent on access to the academic community. The landscape metaphor draws on the notion of a decentered and extended perspective on learning, where mastery is something built into the contours of a landscape, residing in ways of organizing practice, daily routines, and procedures—practices that are embraced rather than focusing on mastering, as a property belonging to particular people (Nielsen, 2008). "This is a landscape in a general sense; not some national park where nature is ideally untouched by human hands, but a cultural landscape inhabited and shaped by human beings through hundreds of thousands of years of practice" (Nelson, 2008, p. 48). To quote Hutchins' description of a distributed perspective on cognition and learning:

> What we try is to move the boundary of the unit of cognitive analysis out beyond the skin of the individual. Doing this enables us to describe the cognitive properties of culturally constructed technical and social systems. (Hutchins, 1995, p. 287)

Accordingly, we look for research resources in a landscape shaped by many years of research practice, cultural traditions, and routines. For the students, apprenticeship in the research landscape is a process of both learning the craft and developing a researcher identity, a sense of belonging and a place to be (Wegener & Tanggaard, 2013). Likewise, supervisors encounter learning experiences that shape their subjectivities and identities (Halse, 2011). They too still explore the landscape.

The above landscape metaphor and the apprenticeship perspective does indeed suggest that learning is not only a cognitive process of information processing or knowledge acquisition (an epistemological process) but more fundamentally an ontological process, an essential part of becoming somebody, an identity-constitutional process of taking part in a changing social practice (Packer & Goicoechea, 2000). Accordingly, learning the craft of research requires access to the communities of practice within research; trying out a distinct way of living; learning the "tips and tricks of the trade"; and living, feeling, and thinking as a researcher. Additionally, new spaces and places within the landscape can continually be explored. Researchers are not bound within set boundaries of research communities or traditions, and new territories are always there to be explored. This is, of course, not just exciting adventurousness and investigation. Kamler and Thomson (2014) note how the journey metaphor is potentially counter-productive and claim that in many doctoral advice books there is a lack of recognition of the identity work involved—especially in doctoral text production. Thus, the novice, still an alien unfamiliar with the history, discussions, and power relations in the field, must both engage in what may be relevant, ignore what may be irrelevant (to save time and not become too distracted), be critical to the masters, *and* avoid missing the substantive/classic debates and terms. Scary!

A Question of Belonging

From the point of view of apprenticeships, developing an identity as a researcher is a question of belonging—of being familiar with a tradition and the cultural styles and norms embraced by the inhabitants in the landscape—and of recognizing what makes a master; yet it is also a question of learning and developing one's own style. As Dreyfus (2001) stresses in his discussion of apprenticeship, one should avoid becoming a copy of one's teacher if one entertains any hope of developing one's own style. Yet it is generally necessary to train with several masters rather than try to go it alone. Thus it is through the old that new things grow. The concept of apprenticeship is particularly suited to illustrating this view of research creativity and innovation, as long as we avoid revering those unfortunate, overly conservative forms of apprenticeship—such as can be found all too easily in research milieu (see Tanggaard, 2014).

Apprenticeship Pedagogy

Based on the work of Lave and Wenger (1991) and Kvale (1999), we argue that apprenticeship learning is situated in diverse forms of local production in the cultural landscape of research. Doctoral training can be compared to learning the craft of research, and from our viewpoint this unfolds through the production of specific articles for trade, with the master representing the status of mastership to be aspired to and emulated by the apprentices. All of this requires intense involvement in real research and it is very difficult to teach somebody how to do it. The process entails a broader embodied and materialized practice involving particular technologies along with joy, suffering, excitement, failure, experiment and discussion, collaboration, and feelings of insecurity. It is first and foremost a daily affair. If considered as a method, it is a matter of being together with other researchers, doing research and living, feeling, thinking, and acting as a researcher. Hasrati (2005) and Lee and Roth (2003) argue that the concept of legitimate peripheral participation is a productive tool for understanding the nature of the doctoral learning process and the relationship between students and supervisors. The main characteristics of this perspective are that novices are supported and given enough credibility to be considered legitimate members of their target communities and are gradually given more demanding activities so as to learn the craft. Similarly, Walker et al. (2008) in their book about rethinking doctoral education, devote a chapter to reconsidering apprenticeship, arguing that apprenticeship pedagogy entails revealing the professional expertise that is all too often taken for granted.

This present book aims to support the supervisor who wants to create such transparency by deliberately constructing occasions and assignments that allow the student to practice key tasks. Additionally, it aims to support the student who wants to co-create learning opportunities. The book also recommends an organizational approach to apprenticeship, which avoids the unintended consequences of pairing a student with a single advisor. As such, a sound apprenticeship process is a matter not just of "good chemistry" between supervisor and student but of providing access to the real practice of conducting research, inviting in, opening up the field, and thereby providing direction as well as keeping the relationship fluid and flexible. In this sense, human doing and knowing are flexible engagements with the world entailing "open-ended processes of improvisation with the social, material, and experiential resources at hand" (Lave, 1993/2009, p. 204). Lave argues that there are no fixed boundaries between an activity and its settings; between cognitive, bodily, and social forms of activity; and between problems and solutions (Lave, 1988). In her 1988 book on thought in practice, Jean Lave asserts that cognitive functionalism and various types of constructionism characterized by homogenous cognitive functions have been and continue to be influential in pedagogical theory as the basis of the Western world's cultivation of pure, abstract thought. This vision of pure, abstract thought is molded from scientific rationality and logic, symbolized by the narrative of the isolated genius. It also stands in immediate contrast to the practical, concrete, contextual, everyday thought exemplified by the diverse kinds of doctoral training discussed in this book.

Learning contexts—traditionally conceived as bounded containers such as schools or universities—have been reconceptualized by situated learning (Lave & Wenger, 1991) as more fluid and relational (Edwards, Biesta, & Thorpe, 2009). In this light, the "landscape" is a metaphor running through the chapters. In this sense, landscapes of learning are realized by both students and supervisors, molded by the existing landscapes of research practices being transformed by the learning that takes place. Engeström (2009, p. 312) describes the research landscape "as a terrain of activity to be dwelled in and explored." The terrain has existing trails, as well as landmarks and boundaries made by others, and when new dwellers enter the terrain, they both follow dominant trails and struggle to thread unconventional paths.

A Pedagogy of Doing

Thus, this book is based on the concept of research as a social practice, which is first and foremost learned precisely as such. However, it is also basically a theoretical perspective concerned with adding materiality, objects, and given tasks to the relational space between supervisor and student. This implies an approach of knowing as doing. As argued by Brinkmann and Tanggaard (2012), we see with our eyes, but take with our hands. Experiencing the world—and knowing it—is a function of our practical activities, of our handling the world and the landscapes we inhabit. What we experience and know about the world are primarily aspects of things that we interact with and manipulate (literally "operate with our hands"). Accordingly, we argue that experimentation, training with real material, and an adequate amount and level of feedback can be viewed as a pedagogy of doing in the landscape of research, which serves as a basis for productive researcher training. No human being is able to be creative or original "out of the blue." The basis for creativity and original work by the student is not flexibility in a vacuum but is found in the ability to dig deep within a particular field and travel the landscape, which requires considerable time and hard work. It is equally important to focus on how to cultivate "student-negotiated agency" (Jazvac-Martek, Chen, & McAlpine, 2011, p. 34), and this book proposes several ideas for adding materiality and experimentation to the doctoral journey. We thus advocate complementary strategies to the student–supervisor relationship and address the doctoral endeavor in a situated context in which a range of relationships are seen as significant (Hopwood, 2010; D. Maher et al., 2008; Maher, Fallucca, & Mulhern Halasz, 2013).

Numerous empirical studies refer to the potential for such pedagogical space for learning in practice. On the basis of research into vocational education in Norway and questionnaire responses from 1,617 students, Mjelde (2001) notes that students experience meaningfulness in learning in the context of workshop-based teaching at the vocational college, in which thought and action are closely integrated. Students experience this despite the unpredictable working hours, large workload, and lack of around-the-clock supervision. Production processes determine how learning progresses in both constructive and less constructive ways, precisely as when a deadline for a paper makes us work harder; we learn from this, without having learning as our main objective. This is an interesting study because it shows that motivation for learning is associated with transparent goals and purpose illuminated in the practices in which one participates. Mjelde points to Vygotsky's and Dewey's experiments on workshop teaching in her argument in favor of the value of practical learning. She highlights Vygotsky's criticism of traditional classroom-based teaching as paying insufficient attention to the fact that learning takes place when acting alongside more competent others.

Likewise, Elmholdt (2006) has studied reproductive, reconstructive, and innovative aspects of apprenticeship. He notes, for example, how young apprentices at a shipyard develop a new and productive solution to a welding problem in the journeymen's absence. This suggests that the delegation of responsibility to young employees or to students in a research practice can promote creativity at the workplace because the master's and journeymen's absence "forces" the young employees or students to find their own solution and provides the space necessary to embolden them to discover solutions that they believe are better than those that already exist.

Moving Away From Pure Learning

The pedagogy associated with these learning situations in practice is, however, simply of an integrated, often implicit, and quite silent sort. We could thus hypothesize that learning is best when one is unaware that one is learning but instead concentrates on *the object* of learning. Modern, frequently cognitive, psychology-inspired learning research is often preoccupied with identifying general procedures, rules, and strategies for learning as well as good, yet general, teaching strategies. Learning is regarded as a pure form that can be described independent of content. In the following, we briefly consider why learning is usually regarded as independent of content and not as a question of learning something specific in a given practice.

The idea that a pure form of learning can and should be cultivated, separate from the concrete subject matter, is historically associated with Kant's idea that there exists a kind of "'pure reason" (cf. *Critique of Pure Reason*). This pure reason concerns rationality in its pure form, which Kant regards as a priori to and within the principle, independent of content. Everything we experience, argues Kant, must be given form by pure reason's perspectives (time and space) and from its categories (for instance, causality). According to Kant, it is the experiencing subject who attributes forms to the sensory material.

Plato

In the Ancient Greek philosophy of Plato we find the concept of abstract "'pure forms," independent of concrete contents. Plato regards these forms as eternal and unchanging "Ideas" that underlie and provide form to people's concrete experiences of a changeable world. Whereas Plato ascribes Ideas to the order of the outer world, Kant feels that pure forms should be understood as belonging to the functions of the mind, a conception that lives on in today's various forms of cognitive research. In much of psychological cognitive research, it is assumed that the human mind functions by reflecting an outer world in which symbolic mental representations are *content* that is processed and *formed* in accordance with more or less fixed rules regarding symbolic manipulation. In artificial intelligence research, such rules are called algorithms. Other terms for these mental forms include diagrams, scripts, and frames (Kyllingsbæk, Harms, & Larsen, 2007).

The Dualism of Form and Content

Within pedagogical research and educational practice, the dualism between form and content has been expressed in various ways. One expression has arisen in the area of pedagogical research that has been directly inspired by cognitive research. The aim of pedagogy becomes to guide teaching toward people's posited "pure" capacity for symbolic manipulation, independent of what the symbols represent, and it is conceptualized, for instance, as a kind of meta-learning or as "learning to learn." This is evident, for example, in Ivar Bjørgen's (1995) presentation of the idea of responsibility for one's own learning in which learning to take responsibility for one's own learning becomes pedagogy's more or less contentless goal. Another expression is present in the numerous varieties of constructivist learning research, often with direct reference to Kant. One criticism of the concept of a pure form of learning focuses on the differentiation between form and content as well as on the problematic separation of mind and body. Dreyfus and Dreyfus (1986) and Dreyfus (2001) have highlighted the problems with cognitive functionalism, the basic premises of which, as with constructivism, stretch back to Descartes and Kant. Cognitive functionalism has been embodied in practice through the efforts to develop artificial intelligence, in which computers are regarded as capable of simulating human cognitive functions.

The Dualism of Body and Mind

Dreyfus (2001) places particular doubt on the distinction between mind and body. In a critical analysis in 2001 of the potential of e-learning, Dreyfus points to Nietzsche's critique of Plato and Christianity, in which Nietzsche comments that the most important element of human life is not our intellectual capacity but, rather, the emotional and intuitive capacities of our bodies. Freedom from the body, postulated through the idea of purely cognitive structures and pure learning, could thus represent a veritable Achilles' heel for cognitive-oriented research. Dreyfus (2001, p. 7) notes that it is our emotional, intuitive, situated, vulnerable, and corporeal existence that permits us to distinguish between the relevant and the less relevant as well as to get a handle on those things with which we occupy ourselves. We could not experience relevance, reality, and meaning without a body, and even if we could, we would be left with very few capabilities indeed.

To regard learning as a corporeal process rooted in social practice in landscapes of learning in the research practice is thus quite different from regarding learning as an individual, constructed process. Furthermore, it has deep implications for our understanding of what kinds of practice and learning are relevant for doctoral students. It forces us to move the perspective toward a broader sense of resources in doctoral training, looking toward much more than the resources found in formal training, PhD courses, and formal supervision. It addresses both the learning landscape in the cultural landscapes of research as well as the unique, subjective experience of doctoral students forcing us to see doctoral education as a journey of identity constitution, becoming someone and getting a sense of what doctoral training implies and what it might become if the resources are extended into the wider landscape.

Good Advice for the PhD Student

- Make sure to get the best out of the research landscape you are now part of.
- Take responsibility for organizing your own learning trajectories, explore the territory, and be aware of the many learning resources besides the relation to your supervisor.
- Scan the research landscape for participation opportunities and try out different relations and collaborations both inside and outside your institution and field of research. A diversity of involvement makes it easier to select and deselect, thus escaping people and activities that make you feel bad, sad, or bored.
- Try to avoid the anxiety related to ambitions of originality by accepting that becoming part of the existing landscapes of research is the first step. Developing your own style is the next step.

Good Advice for the Supervisor

- Encourage the student to explore the wider landscape of learning beyond what she might learn from you.
- Allow for transparency by deliberately constructing occasions and assignments that allow the student to practice key tasks.
- Invite the student into plans beyond dissertation completion, such as co-authorship, shared conference participation, or funding applications.
- Discuss with your student the possible career trajectories and seek out together work tasks and research outlets (conferences, journals) that support a desired trajectory beyond the dissertation work.
- If the student does not thrive, go into dialogue beyond goal-setting strategies. Do not accept the frequently used solution put forward by exhausted doctoral students that "I just need to pull myself together." If this was the solution, it would have been executed.
- Avoid copying the worst practices involved in your own doctoral training. Develop your own supervisor style by keeping a learning mindset intact. Learn from your mistakes; learn from your students; and share your learning experiences with them.

Conclusion

In this chapter, we have introduced the theoretical ideas behind this book. They are related to notions of apprenticeship learning and our perspective on research as unfolding in cultural landscapes. In these landscapes, resources for learning for both doctoral students and their supervisors are widely distributed in the ongoing research practices. In more practical terms, this involves a very hands-on approach as to what it means to be a doctoral student, underlining this as being about much more than just individual readiness and skills accumulation. We thus stress a distributed notion of apprenticeship that opens the door to a wide landscape of resources available for both students and supervisors. Master–student relationships are potentially everywhere. What we must do is seek them out, try them out, and craft them in creative ways. The following chapters will lead the way.

References

Bjørgen, I. A. (1995). *Ansvar for egen læring*. [Responsible for one's own learning]. Trondheim: Tapir Forlag.

Brinkmann, S. (2012). *Qualitative inquiry in everyday life: Working with everyday life materials*. London: Sage.

Brinkmann, S., & Tanggaard, L. (2010). The epistemology of the hand—putting pragmatism to work. In P. Gibbs (Ed.), *Learning, work and practice: New understandings* (147–163). Netherlands: Springer.

Cerwonka, A., & Malkki, L. H. (2008). *Improvising theory: Process and temporality in ethnographic fieldwork*. London: University of Chicago Press.

Collins, A., Brown, J. S., & Newman, S. E. (1989). Cognitive apprenticeship: Teaching the craft of reading, writing, and mathematics. In L. B. Resnick (Ed.), *Knowing, learning, and instruction: Essays in honor of Robert Glaser* (pp. 453–494). Hillsdale, NJ: Lawrence Erlbaum Associates.

Delamont, S. (2009). The only honest thing: Autoethnography, reflexivity and small crises in fieldwork. *Ethnography and Education, 4*(1), 51–63.

Dennen, V. P. (2004). Cognitive apprenticeship in educational practice: Research on scaffolding, modeling, mentoring, and coaching as instructional strategies. In D. H. Jonassen (Ed.), *Handbook of research on educational communications and technology* (2nd ed., pp. 813–828). Mahwah, NJ: Lawrence Erlbaum Associates.

Dewey, J. (1925). *Experience and nature*. Chicago: Open Court.

Dreyfus, H. (2001). *On the internet*. New York: Routledge.

Dreyfus, H., & Dreyfus, S. (1986). *Mind over machine*. New York: The Free Press.

Edwards, R., Biesta G., & Thorpe, M. (2009). *Rethinking contexts for learning and teaching: Communities, activities and networks.* London and New York: Taylor & Francis.

Elmholdt, C. (2006). Innovative learning is not enough. In E. Antonacopolou, P. Jarvis, V. Andersen, B. Elkjaer, & S. Høyrup Pedersen (Eds.), *Learning, working and living: Mapping the terrain of working life learning* (pp. 93–116). London: Palgrave Macmillan.

Engeström, Y. (2009). The future of activity theory: A rough draft. In A. Sannino, H. Daniels, & K. D. Gutiérrez (Eds.), *Learning and expanding with activity theory* (303–328). Cambridge: Cambridge University Press.

Halse, C. (2011). 'Becoming a supervisor': The impact of doctoral supervision on supervisors' learning. *Studies in Higher Education, 36*(5), 557–570.

Hasrati, M. (2005). Legitimate peripheral participation and supervising Ph.D. students. *Studies in Higher Education, 30*(5), 557–570.

Hopwood, N. (2010). A sociocultural view of doctoral students' relationships and agency. *Studies in Continuing Education, 32*(2), 103–117.

Hutchins, E. (1995). *Cognition in the wild.* Cambridge, MA: MIT Press.

Jazvac-Martek M., Chen S., & McAlpine L. (2011). Tracking the doctoral student experience over time: Cultivating agency in diverse spaces. In L. McAlpine & C. Amundsen (Eds.), *Doctoral education: Research-based strategies for doctoral students, supervisors and administrators* (pp. 17–36). London: Springer.

Kamler B., & Thomson, P. (2006). *Helping doctoral students write: Pedagogies for supervision.* London: Routledge.

Kamler, B., & Thomson, P. (2008). The failure of dissertation advice books: Toward alternative pedagogies for doctoral writing. *Educational Researcher, 37*(8), 507–514.

Kamler, B., & Thomson, P. (2014). *Helping doctoral students write: Pedagogies for supervision.* Oxon: Routledge.

Kvale, S. (1999). Forskere i lære [Researcher apprenticeship]. In K. Nielsen & S. Kvale (Eds.), *Mesterlære: Læring som social praksis* [Apprenticeship: Learning as a social practice] (pp. 178–198). Copenhagen: Hans Reitzels Forlag.

Kyllingsbæk, S., Harms, L., & Larsen, A. (2007). Kognitionspsykologi. [Cognitive psychology]. In B. Karpatschof & B. Katzenelson (Eds.), *Klassisk og moderne psykologisk teori* [Classical and modern psychological theory] (pp. 251–272). Copenhagen: Hans Reitzels Forlag.

Lave J. (1993/2009). The practice of learning. In K. Illeris (Ed.), *Contemporary theories of learning: Learning theorists in their own words* (pp. 200–208). London and New York: Routledge.

Lave, J. (1988). *Cognition in Practice.* Cambridge: Cambridge University Press.

Lave, J., & Kvale, S. (1995). What is anthropological research? An interview with Jean Lave by Steinar Kvale. *Qualitative Studies in Education, 8,* 219–228.

Lave, J., & Wenger, E. (1991). *Situated learning: Legitimate peripheral participation.* Cambridge: Cambridge University Press.

Lee S., & Roth W.-M. (2003). Becoming and belonging: Learning qualitative research through legitimate peripheral participation. *Forum Qualitative Sozialforschung/Forum: Qualitative Social Research, 4.*

Maher, D., Seaton, L., McMullen, C., Fitzgerald, T., Otsuji, E., & Lee, A. (2008). "Becoming and being writers": The experiences of doctoral students in writing groups. *Studies in Continuing Education, 30*(3), 263–275.

Maher, M., Fallucca, A., & Mulhern Halasz, H. (2013). Write on! through to the Ph.D.: Using writing groups to facilitate doctoral degree progress. *Studies in Continuing Education, 35*(2), 193–208.

Mills, C. W. (1952/1980). On intellectual craftsmanship. *Society, 17*(2), 63–70.

Mjelde, L. (2001). *Yrkenes pedagogic—fra arbejde til læring, fra læring til arbeid.* Oslo: Yrkeslitteratur as.

Nielsen, K. (2008). The learning landscape of art and craft. In K. Nielsen, S. Brinkmann, C. Elmholdt, L. Tanggaard, P. Museaus, & G. Kraft (Eds.), *A qualitative stance: Essays in honor of Steinar Kvale.* Aarhus: Aarhus Universitetsforlag.

Nielsen, K., Brinkmann, S., Elmholdt, C., Tanggaard, L., Museaus, P., & Kraft, G. (Eds.). (2008). *A Qualitative Stance: Essays in honor of Steinar Kvale.* Aarhus: Aarhus Universitetsforlag.

Nielsen, K., & Tanggaard, L. (2011). Apprenticeship rehabilitated in a postmodern world? *Journal of Vocational Education & Training, 63*(4), 563–573.

Packer, M. J., & Goicoechea J. (2000). Sociocultural and constructivist theories of learning: Ontology, not just epistemology. *Educational Psychologist, 35.*

Tanggaard, L. (2014). *Fooling around: Creative learning pathways.* Charlotte, NC: Information Age Publishers.

Tanggaard, L. & Brinkmann, S. (2008). Til forsvar for en uren pædagogik. *Nordisk Pedagogik, 28*(4), 303–314.

Walker, G. E., Golde, C. M., Jones, L., Bueschel, A. C., & Hutchins, P. (2008). *The formation of scholars: Rethinking doctoral education for the twenty-first century.* San Francisco, CA: Jossey-Bass.

Wegener, C., & Tanggaard, L. (2013). Supervisor and student co-writing: An apprenticeship perspective. *Forum Qualitative Sozialforschung, 14,* 3.

Zuckerman, H. (1997). *Scientific elite.* New York: Free Press.

Chapter Two

Matching Student and Research Community

Abstract

Purpose: The purpose of the present chapter is to describe and analyze examples of successful and not-so-successful matching of students and supervisor in doctoral training.

Central message: The chapter challenges the notion of individual talent as the only sign of research potential. The term *matching* indicates that research talent is and must be relationally defined as a match between requirements in the research community and what the doctoral students bring along and develop as part of their participation.

Takeaways: Supervision relationships that are open and fluid, leading to a "negotiated order" model of supervision where the expectations between supervisor and student are open to change, are of huge value in doctoral training. Students value those supervisors who foster a sense of collegiality and who facilitate the interchange of ideas with other research students.

Keywords: Matching, research talent, "negotiated order model" of supervision, transactional functionality, the right match, reciprocal trust, mismatch and rematch.

Successful and Unsuccessful Matching

One of the most defining moments in a research career is getting access to a research community fitting one's interests. It may seem relatively easy at first sight. Look for the right spot and then just go ahead. However, if one ends up in the wrong place at the wrong time, individual talent and ambitions will make no difference. And what appeared in the first place to be the right spot may not be so eventually. The matching and getting access is a constant negotiation process, not happening in one instance but evolving over time, as the doctoral student gradually becomes a more involved participant in the research community.

In this chapter, examples of successful and not so successful matching will be touched upon. As may already be apparent, the chapter in itself challenges the notion of individual talent as the only sign of research potential. On the contrary, using the term *matching* indicates that talent is and must be relationally defined as a match between requirements in the research community and what the doctoral students bring along and develop as part of their participation (Barab & Plucker, 2002). By matching, we don't necessarily mean the kind of matching opportunities offered by dating sites built on the premise that matching can be realized by listing a set of competences and capabilities and then matching them with another profile. In the real life of research, the matching is a bit more complicated (as it is also in the world of love). The matching more likely resembles a kind of constant negotiation than a once-and-for-all perfect matching. As mentioned by Brinck (2014), in his dissertation on fieldwork and learning in the world of jamming, research can be compared to traveling a long and winding road: "A road that we'll never get to the end of, an endless road of changing directions and changing questions" (p. 20).

Why Research Talent
Is Relationally Defined and Achieved

Delamont, Atkinson, and Parry (2000) draw upon Bernstein's (1971) distinction of modes of socialization (e.g., positional and personal socialization) in describing the way in which the relationship can develop. Positional socialization suggests that both supervisor and student have identities that are fixed, closed, and explicit. This may lead to a "technical rationality" model of supervision, where the supervisor acts as a manager or director and the student is a passive recipient (Acker, Hill, & Black, 1994, p. 485). Conversely, where personal socialization exists, relationships are more open and fluid and identities are negotiable, leading to a "negotiated order" model of supervision, where the expectations between supervisor and student are open to change (Acker et al., 1994, p. 485). Burns, Lamm, and Lewis (1999) argue that, in education, the multidisciplinary and professional base can mean that students value those supervisors who foster a sense of collegiality and who facilitate the interchange of ideas with other research students similar to the classical descriptions of elite apprenticeship in research (Zuckerman, 1997). However, there is no doubt that the relationship between supervisor and doctoral student is vital to the survival of the student in research life, to the quality of the research training, and for the supervisor, as the growth of her research area is dependent on finding and cultivating talents that may take over her role and responsibilities in the future.

Relational Talents

We live in times in which individual talent, whether inspired or genetically preprogrammed, is lavishly celebrated. For exactly this reason, it is important to pay attention to learning processes, which even highly talented people need in order to gain access to and hold their own in specific contexts. Barab and Plucker (2002) write in an article on the concept of talent that we should do more to investigate the relational aspects of the concept of talent. They follow their own advice by underlining a necessary shift in attention from what they call "smart people" to "smart contexts"; this has the potential to allow a focus on apprenticeship and what we call the dynamic and processual dimensions that are inherent in such concepts as talent, intelligence, and expertise.

Barab and Plucker (2002) argue convincingly that talent should be understood as a transactional functionality, which is an attribute of our behavior in certain contexts. This sounds somewhat technical but simply means that one investigates the means by which talent grows through the provision and acceptance of opportunities in a certain context. Talent is, in this reading, a kind of potentiality that is realized in conjunction with opportunities in the surrounding world. It is this kind of exchange that can also explain the types of teaching that are the precondition for nurturing a specific talent in a given research context. Akre and Ludvigsen (1999) give similar examples based on their investigation of the training of medics in the Norwegian hospital sector. They conclude that learning takes place in give-and-take situations in which the components of access and invitation are absolutely crucial. The experienced doctor must invite the junior doctors "inside"; in turn, the novice medics must be able to accept the invitation and allow themselves to be admitted. The development of the give-and-take situation is not a sudden one but is cultivated; it is also something that can easily be overlooked or hard to discern. It is not just a matter of gaining access initially but a matter of getting access continually and progressively. In this view, there are no intelligent people, only intelligent actions carried out by certain people in contexts that offer the opportunity for such actions to take place. Let us again turn to a specific example that helps to explain the meaning of matching, guidance, and lifelong learning for potential talent in the research world.

Finding the Right Match

Professor Scott G. Isaksen is a pupil under the supervision of Ruth B. Noller, whose moniker is the "mother of the mentor concept." Her special talent for helping others to find their way is thus a perfect example of what we might call "elite apprenticeship." As a professor at Buffalo State University, Noller founded its renowned Creative Studies Program. In a recent issue of the *International Journal for Talent Development and Creativity*, Scott Isaksen (2014) described their mentor relationship. Isaksen writes that he first met Noller when handing in an essay as a student on the program, in 1970. When the essay was returned, it was inscribed with comments, corrections, and reflections that covered more of the page than the essay itself. After the first shock, Isaksen realized that he would in fact be able to learn something from this person. As he writes: "I realised she was serious, astute and someone I wanted to get to know better. Had it not been for Ruth, I would have dropped out of the programme because in truth I was a little worried that this creativity thing would be rather too loose a concept for me" (Isaksen, 2014, p. 155). But Noller was anything but flowery. Her background as a mathematician and engineer was the reason she was employed by the university to design some of the program's first online teaching systems. She was also known for her creativity formula, which simply expressed creativity as a function of K, I, and E (Knowledge, Imagination, and Evaluation).

Isaksen and Noller would go on to develop a special relationship. During Isaksen's first year at college, the two met regularly, and Noller invited him home and had her two sons show him the campus. She gave Isaksen the opportunity to meet the foremost experts on creativity at the time—as long as he took care of logistics for the meetings. Isaksen himself was interested in the teaching profession and Noller talked to him about teaching on several occasions. She ensured that he found his place within the curriculum of the creativity program and challenged him to do research work long before the university had developed a program for training researchers. Later, Noller proposed that Isaksen follow a career in research, and she attended the formal committee session that approved the continuation of their path of common learning. Isaksen writes that he later discovered he was not the only "chosen one" and that Noller had over time taken several students under her wing, with the result that she came to be known as "the mother of mentoring."

Reciprocal Trust

This introductory example of the relation between Noller and Isaksen is by way of illustrating the importance of finding the right match (as Isaksen put it, he could really learn something from her). Seldom is it a question of defining a profile and then instigating a neutral development program, to be administered from a distance, as it were. Rather, it is a question of developing relations that can withstand the test of time.

Hans Hauge, a professor of Nordic Studies at Aarhus University in Denmark, says in an essay that as a student at Aarhus under the supervision of Professor Løgstrup and others, the issue at hand was referred to as the "reciprocal trust" that enables all forms of genuine teaching and learning (Hauge, 2011). This trust involves the teacher's faith in the students' willingness to learn, and the students' faith in the ability of the professors to teach them something. Here, teaching should be understood as entailing anything but a neutral cognitive transfer of knowledge; it is instead an integral element of building relationships over time. The premise for trust is that the pupil recognizes the inequality (in terms of the teacher knowing more) and that at the same time the teacher tries to develop the pupil to become his or her equal. You can learn something from someone only if that person has something you do not possess and would like to possess. Furthermore, this works only if the teacher is interested in the fact that you should learn generally. Hauge writes (2011, p. 110):

> Løgstrup departs from the belief that life exists in itself and in advance of us forming it—which clearly demonstrates his grounding in Grundtvig's philosophy. From him, I gather something about inequality. The teacher has the knowledge that the student lacks. The teacher must consider students as equals, as grown, responsible people who are willing to learn. The teacher must respect the unequal relationship (Løgstrup, 1987, p. 70). The teacher must never force students into "dialogue" or make them give a presentation; students should have the freedom to remain silent, or to be absent. In treating them as equals, there are many who will not understand what is said. This is not the

teacher's problem. The decision is that of the student. And now to the most important part: "The input of two parties is, from a certain point of view, contradictory. That of the student is to recognise the inequality; that of the teacher to remove it." If the student sees the teacher as their equal, everything goes wrong.

Pedagogy is, according to Hauge quoting Løgstrup, carried by trust. "The pupil's trust of the teacher, his or her skills and sincerity; and the teacher's trust of the pupil and of his or her openness and willingness to learn. This reciprocal trust is not something that can be rationalised. It is of a primary character in our being, something we cannot truly investigate but that is a constant in our existence. We cannot exchange or replace it with something else" (Løgstrup, 1987, p. 37). Matching is thus not a mechanical "one-off" process; it builds on reciprocal trust, which is developed over time.

Lene's Story: Is This a Place to Work?

When we began writing this book, the first thing that came to my mind as a survival issue in a PhD project was the notion of matching and the importance of finding the right kind of research environment to do research. I remember Charlotte was very curious: What did I mean, and how could potential students learn from this, and what to do if you find yourself stuck in a research environment unproductive for you?

It is no coincidence that matching came to my mind as one of the most important elements in doctoral training. In my own research journey, this has played a major role. When I studied psychology, I did not think of myself as somebody going to have a life as a researcher. Looking at the professors in the gray halls of the psychology department at Aarhus University, I did not see a stimulating and interesting life. As the years went by, the professors became more and more gray, and not only did their hair turn gray, so did the look in their eyes. As a young student, I found most of the professors looking bored and not really getting anywhere. And so I was keen on getting out of there and finding a working spot full of life, cooperation, and fun. As a student, I found these words (life, joy, fun) to be in quite stark opposition to research. However, when I wrote both my bachelor and my master theses, I had to admit to myself that I loved it. It was full of life and fun. It was also a journey of difficulties, hard times, and not getting anything done, but digging deep into a particular research area was very productive, stimulating, and satisfying to me. My professor at the time—Steinar Kvale, coauthor of the SAGE best-selling book *Inter-Views: Learning the Craft of Qualitative Research Interviewing*—was very instrumental in making it a fun journey for me, and he played a large part in opening my eyes to the potentials of a life as a researcher. He challenged me deeply, and he made me cry because of frustration at having to revise and re-do my text (somehow at that time I thought it could be written directly from a first thought), but the fun part was that it felt as if he invested not only time but interest in my project, and he kept it on track. Whenever I had difficulties in my writing, he told me to write what I had just said to him. Whenever I felt I needed to read more theory, he said: "You have read enough; go write about what you know already." For me, this was the most stimulating of all, giving me the trust that the kind of thinking I was engaged in was worth it. As such, when he asked me if I had thought of doing a PhD, I said (reluctantly) yes.

I knew the match was in place and I was already becoming part of a research community that seemed stimulating, rewarding, and also safe, in the sense of being in a place where things got done, where I could see people were making it. Sadly enough, Steinar Kvale died too young, just 70 years of age, only 14 days after he retired (it is dangerous to stop working), but if he were alive today, he would see the fruits of his work, with many of my co-students, some older, some younger, having made it in the research community (of which he was at times also very critical). The reason for this success (if we accept that getting tenure is equal to success) is quite simple: Steinar was an eminent research environment constructor, deeply interested in how to make a productive research community, believing in research as a way of life. He involved us in research and joint book projects, invited us to his own wedding (opening up to life outside university), insisted that research is something you do not only from 9 to 5 but also when drinking beers in the bar or reading fashion magazines, which he did himself because, as he said, "The fashion world is highly innovative," and he was looking for new trends in these magazines to turn into research objects.

Nowadays, when teaching PhD students on the PhD methods course in qualitative methods (with Professor Svend Brinkmann), I meet a lot of students who have not found the right match. Some of them end up in such situations because they go only for the title and the prestige, not really realizing that research is a way of life. Others end up in a research community where they are not involved in any kind of community, not recognized, and sometimes mostly just doing work the professors need to get done. Sometimes, the only way forward is to get out of there; in other cases the solution lies in having a talk with the supervisor, asking how one might get more involved, get more feedback, finding out how to live a life as a researcher. Realizing that the match is not there, that something needs to be done, is the most important part. But if one has to change, try to search carefully in the first place. Just getting a PhD is not always the right thing, but getting one in a community where things are thrilling, exciting, and enjoyable and worth it is a wonderful experience.

What Is Needed to Find the Match?

Concrete advice for prospective doctoral students and for supervisors looking for the right-fitting candidates is surely to agree on expectations concerning the doctoral period. How much work will be involved; what kinds of expectations exist toward supervision; what is the role of the doctoral student in the research community; and what will the supervisor expect from the student regarding output, contributions to existing research in the community, conference presentations, and so on?

These dialogues about expectations must ideally take place before getting started on the research journey, in the beginning and at regular moments during the process of research training. In most cases the matching attempts take place before the actual doctoral training begins. Supervisors check up on potential students by looking into their writing, publications records, and former activities, while students look at the websites of potential professors, listen to stories from former students, and try to get an impression of the community from the stories told about it. The point is that this is a process that unfolds over time.

As mentioned, we asked some of our colleagues to reflect on their own experiences regarding doctoral training. We encouraged them to write about defining moments along the way. Our colleague, Svend Brinkmann, responded with a story of matching and he describes it as being a matter of not "jumping on the first train" but having the patience to wait for the right one. His story also challenges the notion of defining moments for being a term not having an exhaustive process orientation.

Svend's Story About Jumping on the Right Train

I have problems writing about defining moments, because I don't really believe in them. If we change directions or make a significant choice in our lives, it is because of numerous factors and forces, big and small, which cannot normally be isolated to a single point in time. Instead, I believe in long stretches of work. I believe that what makes a PhD project—as well as an academic career—is a temporally extended process rather than any specific points in that process. It is the process that is defining, not the moments. When we do reflect on our past, for example, as students or supervisors, we can sometimes pinpoint certain moments in hindsight, but these are most often constructed in retrospect, I think. At least, this is how my own life—professionally as well as personally—appears to me, but it is probably different for others. When did I decide to become a psychologist, to pursue an academic career, to formulate a specific research project, and so on? When were the defining moments? I am not really sure.

However, when looking back to the time when I was finishing my master's degree and getting ready to apply for a PhD, I can truly say that I was headed on a different track from where I (fortunately) ended up. I was writing most of my master's thesis while I was a visiting student at Oxford University (associated with the sub-faculty of philosophy), and I knew that the next round of PhD applications at my home university (Aarhus) would be within work and organizational psychology. In agreement with a supervisor, I was drafting a PhD project within this area, but I really felt that I was betraying my own interests. Yes, I was interested in work and organizational life, but in a way that was much more theoretical (and qualitative) than the relevant supervisor wanted. I remember having a conversation with Steinar Kvale—who was to become my actual PhD supervisor—and he asked me: "Are you sure that this is what you want to do? Don't waste your talents!"

After this I threw my PhD application away. I wrote a new one based on my philosophical ideas about the relations between morality and psychology. The new one was a much more risky project (normally, theoretical projects did not—and still do not—get funded), and I had to wait until there was an open call for PhD applications. I ended up obtaining funding for my con amore project, and with Steinar Kvale as supervisor. I could probably have done a decent job in the other area, but I would have needed to restrict myself in many different ways. And I wouldn't have been given the chance to have Steinar Kvale as my main supervisor and mentor. And then my life would probably have looked quite different today.

But can I say that the conversation with Steinar Kvale was a defining moment? Perhaps. But it quite simply brought home to me what I had known all along. And it is certainly likely that I would have made the same choice even without Steinar urging me to think twice. Still, the conversation has remained in my memory for a reason, along with other fond memories of Steinar, and I sometimes think of it when I need to remind myself about the importance of patience. Sometimes (perhaps quite often) one should not jump on board the first train that comes along.

In this matching story, we get the impression of at least two kinds of matching: one kind concerning the theme of research and the interest of the potential student, and the other concerning the relationship between the student and the potential PhD supervisor. This is an important distinction as it calls for two kinds of necessary matching ambitions on behalf of the doctoral student—finding the right theme and finding the right place, although these may also go hand in hand. Which is most important? Well, this depends. While Svend went for his con amore project, I (Lene) ended up with a con amore research topic (apprenticeship learning). It was part of a state-financed research project with very particular aims, which I sometimes felt was simultaneously restricting my focus and keeping me on the right track, partly con amore, partly something done on behalf of others, directed at particular state interests (learning more about apprenticeship training and learning in Denmark), but I knew my supervisors would carry me through this. It was not purely con amore, so I actually relied a lot on my potential supervisors and had confidence that they were the right fit for me.

Mismatch

The above ideas of matching as being a process, a relational dance, negotiation or coordination, jumping on the right train at the right time, judging if the research community is a place to live a life, and wondering whether you can see yourself there calls for images of scientific craftsmanship that destroy distinctions between work and life. As stated by Ingold, "There is no division, in practice, between work and life. [An intellectual craft] is a practice that involves the whole person, continually drawing on past experience as it is projected into the future" (Ingold, 2001, p. 240, as cited in Brinkmann, 2012, p. 4).

Indeed, matching happens when expectations informed by history and past experiences get transformed in actual time into feelings of belonging, having found a place, acquiring a research identity; it is understood as a subjective feeling of belonging in a certain place (Dreier, 2008). However, as smooth and happy as this process might be, it can also develop into a mismatch. The following story from one of our colleagues, Rasmus Birk, highlights the trouble with matchmaking and the feelings and some of the potential learning this experience resulted in for him.

Rasmus's Story About Mismatch

It is Monday morning; I have just gotten off the train and gone into the office of the company sponsoring my doctoral research. On my way to grab the day's first cup of coffee, I run into my manager; she looks directly at me and asks me if I have "five minutes to talk." My heart starts racing, for some reason. We sit down and my manager starts talking:

We worked a really long time to get a PhD here in the company, and we really looked forward to you coming. But after these first two months, it has become apparent to us that your research methods are disturbing to our working procedures. For this reason we're hereby terminating your contract, effective immediately.

Stunned, my heart racing, I ask if there's any possibility that we can discuss this. "No," is the short answer. I ask her to specify the reason for firing me; how exactly was I "disturbing"; what did I do wrong? She repeats her phrase from before; apparently my qualitative study is "disturbing working procedures," something I had not personally experienced in any way. Struggling to keep myself composed and not to start crying, my voice trembles as I say, "I find it very frustrating, that you're not willing to talk to me at all, and elaborate on this." My—now former—manager looks at me and simply says, "I hear what you're saying. But you're still fired. I want your key and then I'd like to ask you to leave."

I take the train home.

So what, exactly, happened here? I am still not sure. I was employed by the private company as a doctoral student, in collaboration with a university. They had hired me to do a qualitative research project about their business practices. I had been working on the project for a couple of months at this point, doing mainly participant observation—as I was employed at the company and shared an office with my colleagues, it is difficult not to do participant observation. My job was to produce research about best practices and what worked especially well in this particular company. We had, in the initial meetings, agreed that these practices should be investigated qualitatively. That is, I should produce research and not just evaluations, or worse, research with predetermined conclusions. Sitting in a meeting with my future boss, my supervisor-to-be and I had presented a qualitative framework to which they wholly agreed. Indeed, my manager had enthusiastically agreed with my initial description of the project and even said that it was entirely consistent with her idea of how best to investigate the field. I wanted to do an ethnography of the organization. I wanted to do interviews and observations and document analysis, and I wanted to consider everything as data, as reading Bruno Latour had taught me. As my initial tale tells, I did not get that far. To this day, I am not sure what happened. I never got another explanation. Perhaps I really *was* disturbing their work. Perhaps I had not properly conveyed to my manager that qualitative research potentially "disturbs" or slightly shifts current practices when people reflect upon what they do. But most of the time, at least, I had spent sitting in my office reading and preparing for the "real" field study, which was to start later in the year. So it doesn't really fit. Perhaps I was fired for not doing enough? Maybe she was stressed and making irrational decisions; maybe the company was strapped for cash?

In their request for PhD stories, Charlotte and Lene asked what this episode means to me now. I am not entirely sure about this, either. I am a doctoral student again. I don't think about this episode much anymore, and I don't mention it very often either. It is an odd story to tell, and it takes a while too. After the first months, I grew tired of it. I have lived through most doctoral students' biggest nightmare—*failing*, being deemed not good enough, being *fired*. But I survived; the world kept turning; and people went about their business, and in the end the worst was probably the fear that I had missed my opportunity of being in academia. Turns out I had not. Instead I had the opportunity to scrutinize and think it through again—did I really want to do a PhD? For me, the answer turned out to be yes. To conclude: I don't know that I can say that I learned something from this absurd experience, other than that failing dramatically in one's doctoral research is not, thankfully, the end of the world. What does the episode mean to me now? Probably that I am a little bit insane—or dedicated—to trying this endeavor again.

Failing Is Not the End of the World

Here, the question is one of a definite mismatch, or disconnect, which it was best to sever. As it occurred early in his doctoral training, Rasmus continued to explore his PhD options and was eventually fortunate enough to find the right supervisor and the right place to be. The research community in this private company did not appear to recognize the kind of research the student aimed for, and other things might have happened. The good part of the story is that the student actually survived and found that failing is not the end of the world—a useful competency for all doctoral students when facing rejections or harsh reviews after months of paper writing. But most importantly, he learned how dedicated he was to pursue a research career. As the story concludes, this is maybe what he learned from failing. Hopefully, the company also learned a few lessons concerning the role of matching and its own expectations toward doctoral students and the importance of highlighting and explaining these before the study proceeds. While a mismatch is nothing to go for specifically, it points at the importance of breaking up, finishing something that does not work. However, in competitive times, this may not happen due to pressure on students to finish very quickly.

Finishing on Time?

Today, research is a very competitive game. Since the source and volume of research studentships gained and the number of doctoral degrees awarded are strong factors in assessing the quality of an institution's research climate, B. M. Grant (2005, p. 344) argues that this has placed increased pressure on academics to ensure that students finish on time and "privileges the rational specification of process (services) and product." Many students expect a quick fix, and supervisors may be compelled to over-direct students' development in order to meet the demands imposed by external bodies (Deuchar, 2008, p. 490). In the field of education this may cause tension, given the recognition that a flexible approach to research supervision is required in order to attend to the multiplicity of student needs.

Research supervisors clearly face increasing complexity surrounding the skills and expertise they are expected to have and the style of supervision they are anticipated to adopt. Building on earlier research in supervisory styles (Delamont et al., 2000; B. Grant & Graham, 1994; Kam, 1997; Pearson and Brew, 2002), Gatfield and Alpert (2002) have extracted two dimensions upon which supervision styles have been arrayed, namely "structure" and "support." From these emerge four paradigms of supervision styles in relation to the supervisor's perceived roles in the organization and management of the research project, supporting the candidate and resourcing the research project. The *laissez-faire* style makes the assumption that candidates are capable of managing both the research project and themselves; the *pastoral* style assumes that they are able to manage the project but may need personal support; the *directorial* style assumes that they need support in managing the project but not themselves; and the *contractual* style suggests that supervisors and students need to negotiate the extent of the support in both project and personal terms (Taylor & Beasley, 2005).

Understanding these styles can help both doctoral students and supervisors when looking for better matching or searching for reasons why the matching attempts go wrong. Hasrati (2005, p. 558) highlights a possibly related concept of cognitive apprenticeship, whereby supervisors *model* by "making explicit their tacit knowledge"; *coach* by "supporting students at doing the tasks"; and, finally, *fade* when they have "empowered the students to continue independently." Supervisors may also use a scaffolding procedure where they provide more support to students in the initial stages of their research but expect them to become more independent later on. This may be particularly important in a research environment that is individualistic in nature and where the lack of a critical mass of scholars in a particular area often means that research is conducted in relative isolation (Parry & Hayden, 1999). In the following, Ninna Meier, tells a story about a mismatch between her supervisor and herself as a doctoral student and between the two identities as an employee with certain rights and at the same time a doctoral student seen first and foremost as a brain working 24/7.

Ninna's Story About Finishing on Time

It is early September and I have the first supervision meeting since I came back from my leave of absence as a primary caregiver to my mother, who died of brain cancer in April. May and June went by in a haze, and although I have been back, my fixed deadline is rapidly approaching and I have not gotten much constructive work done. I am meeting my two supervisors—a primary supervisor and a co-supervisor—and I have requested that they are both present, as the communication between me and my primary supervisor is problematic, to put it diplomatically. I want to terminate the supervision relationship, as I feel he doesn't understand the field my work is moving into and that he wants to direct it into a different direction, where I don't see the primary relevance and do not want to contribute. We cannot have any constructive discussions about this; any attempts to do this end in him angrily raising his voice and me not listening. At the meeting in my co-supervisor's office, he attempts to mediate between us, but without results. At one point I say in desperation: "Will you at least agree that the way you say something to me will affect the way I hear it?" "No," he says, angrily, "how you hear things that's your problem, not mine." I am dumbfounded; "what can I do?," I think, "when we cannot even agree on this?" "Also," he adds, "you are not nearly as far along as you should have been at this point in time. I had expected you to have written quite a bit more at this time. You really need to pick up the pace, if you're going to meet your deadline." I am furious and barely able to refrain from saying "Well, excuse me, in case you haven't noticed I have been busy caring for my dying mum!" Instead I say, "I don't see how this is going to work. I don't want you as my supervisor anymore." After the meeting I talk to my co-supervisor, who's now my primary and only supervisor: "I agree," he says diplomatically, "it is not constructive between you two." A few months later I am presenting a paper at a research seminar in the department, where I am a visiting PhD student. As usual, after the presentation people comment on the paper and suggest different changes that could improve it, mostly in the form of "Oh, I thought of this interesting paper by XXX, maybe you should read this!" or "You could look into theory XXX!" I jot down all the different suggestions, but then one of the participants says: "This is all very nice, but instead of opening all these doors into new directions, let's remember that she has a deadline and discuss how we can best help her improve this paper within the given timeframe." I look at her and think: "That's supervision! How do I get more of that?" After the meeting, I corner her and she agrees to be my co-supervisor for the remaining months, a decision I never regret.

I took several things away from my experiences. First, I was shocked to learn firsthand the consequences of the organization of employment and supervision of PhD students: As an employee, I could contact the HR department and get permission to go on terminal care leave. As a PhD student, I was a brain—a cognitive resource that was expected to work 100% the day I started working again. No one, none of my supervisors or my department head, had a talk with me about different ways of getting back to work again. I just received an e-mail informing me, that now that I was back to work (two weeks after funeral), the PhD deadline was in effect again: The clock was ticking. So, when my supervisor pointed out that he was disappointed in how far along I was, it felt like a slap in the face. Formally, he was right on all accounts: I was not his responsibility, the department head was my personal manager. He was responsible for my academic work and he was right: I needed to pick up the pace. But the way he chose to approach this was not helpful at all.

Why Matching Can Be Difficult

In German, "the supervisor" is translated into "die doctor vater," which means the doctoral father. This underlines the power relation between the two, but also how the supervision relationship can resemble former relationships, leading to feelings of love, hate, gratitude, and frustration. It is clear that the workings of power and identity can provoke particular anxiety among students if the optimal relationship is seen to be one which is built upon collegiality (Burns et al., 1999).

Many students have an image of the ideal supervisor or mentor but in the end come to accept the status quo. This can however result in a failure to address problems. (Deuchar, 2008). It is also evident that some supervisors are strongly influenced by their own experiences of being supervised or their other experiences of supervising at both undergraduate and postgraduate levels. This supports Grant and Grahams's (1999, p. 8) evidence that "shadow figures and relationships" from previous personal and professional experiences may influence the supervision relationship and steer it in a particular direction. Acker argues that most students value a "negotiated order" approach to supervision (Acker et al., 1994, p. 485), where expectations can be revisited at relevant times. They seek a balance between autonomy, ownership, and the need for guidance and support and a flexible supervisor, responsive to the student's needs and driven by an ethos of open communication and a frank exchange of views.

Here, there is a suggestion that it is often the absence of qualities of supervision that cause matching to go awry. Of course, there can also be any number of practical circumstances that hinder a good match, for example a quite specific misfit between the strengths of the student and the demands of the research project. Below, before concluding this chapter on matching, are a few guidelines for both prospective or actual doctoral students and supervisors. These guidelines also summarize the main conclusions of the chapter.

Good Advice for the PhD Student

- Do your research beforehand—check the supervisor and her or his team. What are their records? Have other PhD students finished their studies, and where are they now? If there are too many students, this may be an indication that there will be less time for you, and the research environment may be very competitive as there is less space for each individual student. On the other hand, you can expect a lot of peer-learning and maybe even a thrilling social environment.
- What kinds of research will you be doing? Will you be part of a team or on your own? Consider what you think is best for you and use this as a decisive factor when choosing a research environment.
- Make your priorities—why are you doing your doctoral studies? Are you willing to do the work, to experience some periods of loneliness and writer's block and long periods without immediate feedback and publication pressure?

Good Advice for the Supervisor

- Check the academic history of the student—have they published anything before? This may give you a sense of what the student might still have to learn to fit your own research community.
- Does the student know the craft of research—have they been a research assistant or otherwise part of a research project? This may indicate that the student has learned the basic part of living a researcher's life, and you can get a better start. However, the student might also have acquired bad habits, which might need to be changed.
- Is the student willing to make an effort—do they know what kinds of investment and offerings doctoral training might involve? Look at their résumé and check if they have changed jobs too quickly; do they know what it means to work?
- What is your own supervisory style, and what have you learned so far as a supervisor? How might you use this learning to guide future students?
- Trust your intuition—you will very often know if a potential student can make it; trust the first impression!

Conclusion

This chapter explored the issue of matching and what it requires from both doctoral students and their supervisors. The relationship between student and supervisor/research environment was described as a process, developing over time, and we have highlighted personal stories and research studies concluding that it is a matter of style, figuratively waiting for the right train and looking into former relationships that might explain how one handles the often intense relationship between doctoral student and supervisor as part of research training. The chapter concluded with a few guidelines and advice, which may be of some help for prospective doctoral students and their supervisors. Even if they do not prevent failures and mismatching, which can sometimes be unavoidable, they may allow for more appropriate coping strategies and thus ensure a more fruitful doctoral process for both parties.

References

Acker, S., Hill, T., & Black, E. (1994). Thesis supervision in the social sciences: Managed or negotiated? *Higher Education, 28*, 483–498.

Akre, V., and Ludvigsen, S. (1999). At lære medicinsk praksis [Learning medical practice]. In K. Nielsen & S. Kvale (Eds.), *Mesterlære—Læring som social praksis* [Apprenticeship—Learning as social practice]. Copenhagen: Hans Reitzels Forlag.

Barab, S. A., & Plucker, J. A. (2002). Smart people or smart contexts? Cognition, ability, and talent development in an age of situated approaches to knowing and learning. *Educational Psychologist, 37*(3), 165–182.

Bernstein, B. (1971). *Class, codes and control.* London: Routledge and Kegan Paul.

Brinck. L. (2014). *Ways of the jam: Collective and improvisational perspectives on learning.* PhD thesis. Department of Communication and psychology. Aalborg: Aalborg University. Available at: https://rmc.dk/sites/default/files/uploads/public/forskning_og_udvikling/lars_brinck_ways_of_the_jam_web_0.pdf.

Brinkmann, S. (2012). *Qualitative inquiry in everyday life: Working with everyday life materials.* London: Sage.

Burns, R., Lamm, R., & Lewis, R. (1999). Orientations to higher degree supervision: A study of supervisors and students in education. In A. Holbrook & S. Johnston (Eds.), *Supervision of postgraduate research in education* (pp. 55–74). Australia: Australian Association for Research in Education.

Delamont, S., Atkinson, P., & Parry, O. (2000). *The doctoral experience: Success and failure in graduate school.* London: Falmer Press.

Deuchar, R. (2008). Facilitator, director or critical friend? Contradiction and congruence in doctoral supervision styles. *Teaching in Higher Education, 13*(4), 489–500.

Dreier, O. (2008). Learning in structures of social practice. In S. Brinkmann, C. Elmholdt, G. Kraft, P. Musaeus, K. Nielsen, & L. Tanggaard (Eds.), *A qualitative stance: Essays in honor of Steinar Kvale* (pp. 85–96). Aarhus: Aarhus University Press.

Gatfield, T., & Alpert, F. (2002). The supervisory management styles model. In A. Goody, J. Herrington & M. Northcote (Eds.), *Proceedings of the 2002 Annual International Conference of Higher Education Research and Development Society of Australasia* (pp. 263–273). Perth, Australia: Higher Education Research and Development Society of Australasia.

Grant, B., & Graham, A. (1994). Guidelines for discussion: A tool for managing postgraduate supervision. In O. Zuber-Skerritt and Y. Ryan (Eds.), *Quality in postgraduate education* (pp. 165–177). London: Kogan Page.

Grant, B., & Graham, A. (1999). Naming the game: Reconstructing graduate supervision. *Teaching in Higher Education, 4*(1), 77–89.

Grant, B. M. (2005). Fighting for space in supervision: Fantasies, fairytales, fictions and fallacies. *International Journal of Qualitative Studies in Education, 18*(3), 337–354.

Hasrati, M. (2005). Legitimate peripheral participation and supervising PhD students. *Studies in Higher Education, 30*(5), 557–570.

Hauge, H. (2011). Kritik af ren pædagogik: Fra danskhed til newspeak [Critique of a pure pedagogics]. In T. Rømer, L. Tanggaard, & S. Brinkmann (Eds.), *Uren pædagogik* [Impure pedagogics]. Aarhus: Klim Publishers.

Isaksen, S. G. (2014). A tribute to Dr. Ruth B. Noller. *International Journal for Talent Development and Creativity, 1*(1), 155–156.

Kam, B. H. (1997). Style and quality in research supervision. *Higher Education, 34*(1), 81–103.

Løgstrup, K. E. (1987). *System og symbol: Essays* [System and symbols: Essays]. Copenhagen: Gyldendal.

Parry, S., & Hayden, M. (1999). Experiences of supervisors in facilitating the induction of research higher degree students to fields of education. In A. Holbrook & S. Johnson (Eds.), *Supervision of postgraduate research in education* (pp. 35–53). Coldstream, Victoria: Australian Association for Research in Education.

Pearson, M., & Brew, A. (2002). Research training and supervision development. *Studies in Higher Education, 27*(2), 135–50.

Taylor, T., & Beasley, N. (2005). *A handbook for doctoral supervisors*. London: Routledge.

Zuckerman, H. (1997). *Scientific elite*. New York: Free Press.

Chapter Three

Originality and Contribution

Abstract

Purpose: The purpose of the present chapter is to address how novelty aspirations must be balanced with humbleness and involvement in traditions of the field.

Central message: A creative and original contribution can be achieved by critically using models and knowledge that are already present in the field. First of all, experience and talent take time and hard work.

Takeaways: Creative research can be achieved by means of habits for fine-tuning research skills. Developing habits includes strategies for enhancing experiment; self-reflection; and critical dialogue with others, with theory, and with data.

Keywords: Making an impact, novelty, originality, humbleness, discipline, traditions, habits, powers of expression, voice, practice, moving on to the edge of the box.

Making an Impact

The ambition of making an impact is inherent in the research profession. There is always—also for doctoral students—the issue of playing it safe at the risk of being bland versus taking a high risk and possibly stumbling badly. In our opinion, this is not an either–or proposition. Doctoral research outcomes (oral presentations, papers, and the dissertation) are supposed to live up to some kind of novelty criterion. Like that of any other researcher, your work must deserve an "original" stamp to some degree. In this chapter, we address how novelty aspirations must be balanced with a great deal of humbleness and involvement in routines and traditions. It is often suggested that we must "jump out of the box" to be original. When jumping out of the box, however, the return on investment and time might be limited. Making an original contribution is not a seal of quality in itself. In short, we will address how originality *and* relevance can be achieved through a strategy that could be termed "moving on to the edge of the box" instead of jumping out of it.

"Forced Novelty"

At a recent conference workshop about publishing in peer-reviewed journals, the veteran ethnographer John Van Maanen stated that as an editor and reviewer, he really dislikes manuscript introductions like this: This paper develops a new concept. "What is wrong with the old concepts?" he asked rhetorically and advised new scholars to avoid what he termed "forced novelty." Rather, he encouraged doctoral scholars (and probably also experienced researchers) to tell an interesting story, tell it in a new way, take up an idea, and use it to represent the data analysis as a "'good puzzle'" (Van Maanen, 2013). Likewise, Pillutla and Thau (2013) claim that a focus on the novel reveals a profound misunderstanding of the scientific enterprise and that scholarship should accord primacy to the problem being solved rather than novel theory development.

Changing the conversation as Weick did, however, may not just connote high aspirations. It is more likely to overshadow the fact that creative

---

Changing the Conversation With Weick

In his tribute to Weick, aptly puts it this way: Of all the accomplishments we might attribute to Weick, undoubtedly one of his greatest is that he has, in the modern vernacular, "changed the conversation" of our field. Changing the conversation has become something of an idealistic standard that we like to use to connote high aspirations in counseling PhD students, junior faculty, and even many senior people hoping to leave some legacy. We often say that one's professional goal ought not to be just getting published, but making a difference. That high aspiration has become the hoped for final step in a progressive litany that reads: "You don't just want to be published, you want to be read. You don't just want to be read, you want to be remembered (and, therefore, cited). You don't just want to be cited, you want to change *the conversation.*" (Gioia, 2006, p. 1710) contributions involve time and tradition. Vera John-Steiner writes in her *Notebooks of the Mind*: "In art as well as science, learning that leads to creative work requires an individual to work at it. Creativity lies in the capacity to see more sharply and with greater insight that which one already knows or that which is buried at the margin of one's awareness" (John-Steiner, 1997, pp. 51–52). And furthermore: "The power to select useful models from the past in one's discipline grows as an individual's own talent develops. It takes time and it takes experience" (p. 57). Experience and talent take time and hard work. And still, we all want to be individual, right?

"We're All Individuals"

It would be nice too if someone told us how to achieve this. However, if we pursue individuality by instruction, we are already not that individual. In Monty Python's movie *Life of Brian*, the paradox is aptly captured in this scene in which the crowd pursues a terrified Brian, assuming he is the new Savior:

Brian:	No, no. Please, please, please listen. I've got one or two things to say.
The Crowd:	Tell us! Tell us both of them!
Brian:	Look, you've got it all wrong. You don't need to follow me. You don't need to follow anybody! You've got to think for yourselves! You're all individuals!
The Crowd:	Yes! We're all individuals!
Brian:	You're all different!
The Crowd:	Yes! We're all different!
Man in crowd:	I'm not...
Man in crowd:	Shhh!
Brian:	You've all got to work it out for yourselves.
The Crowd:	Yes! We've got to work it out for ourselves!
Brian:	Exactly!
The Crowd:	Tell us more!
Brian:	No! That's the point! Don't let anyone tell you what to do! Otherwise—Ow! Ow!

There may be times when a supervisor just wants to shout: "Ow! Ow! You've got to work it out for yourselves." And this may be what is needed. As noted by Kroll (2010), supervisors do not need to offer students rigid templates. Rather, they should encourage students to see research methodologies as if they were travel guides, enabling them to explore new frontiers themselves. As addressed in Chapter 1, however, exploring new frontiers is no easy, harmless endeavor. What doctoral students can practice, however, and what supervisors should encourage, is to experiment with strategies for temporarily—yet genuine—letting go of direction and control. The courage to do so can be nurtured by means of apprenticeship strategies. It is thus necessary for research advisors to assist not only the formulation and clarifying of ideas, but also the sense of risk experienced by research students (Barnacle & Dall'Alba, 2014). The point here is clear: You cannot just—and especially not when *asked*—be original. Strategies, advice, and collaboration for specific reasons are needed in order to balance skills acquisition and the investment of self, including commitment and risk.

We Have to Work It Out Ourselves—But How?

Original ideas often appear as vague images and notions easily overlooked or neglected. However, there are several strategies for fostering, acknowledging, and maintaining impulses, hunches, and whims and ways to keep working with them. All kinds of ideas, personal notes, excerpts from books, written conversations, and outlines of projects can serve to develop what Mills (1952/1980) terms one's "powers of expression." The trick, he states, is to always have so many plans that the question is what to work on next. At the same time, however, it is important to keep track of a master agenda as it keeps the intellectual enterprise under control and guides you in your further reading and in dialogues with colleagues.

Mills suggests setting up a file of personal experience and professional activities, plans, and ideas underway. He points to the fact that accomplished thinkers treat their own minds carefully and keep track of and organize their experiences. The file is a way to develop confidence and thus can become a source of original intellectual work (see the Keeping a File With Mills box).

Traveling Occupied Territory

The journey metaphor does not necessarily support the students' "powers of expression." While the metaphor serves well for encouraging adventurousness resulting in possibly original contributions, it also has constraining side effects.

Keeping a File With Mills

In this file, you, as an intellectual craftsman, will try to get together what you are doing intellectually and what you are experiencing as a person. Here you will not be afraid to use your experience and relate it directly to various works in progress. By serving as a check on repetitious work, your file also enables you to conserve your energy. It also encourages you to capture "fringe-thoughts": various ideas, which may be by-products of everyday life; snatches of conversation overheard on the street; or, for that matter, dreams. Once noted, these may lead to more systematic thinking, as well as lend intellectual relevance to more directed experience.

By keeping an adequate file and thus developing self-reflective habits, you learn how to keep your inner world awake. Whenever you feel strongly about events or ideas, you must try not to let them pass from your mind, but instead formulate them for your files and in so doing draw out their implications to show yourself either how foolish these feelings or ideas are or how they might be articulated into productive shape. The file also helps you build up the habit of writing. You cannot "keep your hand in" if you do not write something at least every week. In developing the file, you can experiment as a writer and thus, as they say, develop your powers of expression. (Mills, 1952/1980, pp. 1–2)

It is important to keep in mind that traveling the landscape does not only involve the exploration of the land; it also involves the exploration of being a traveler—that is, identity work. Kamler and Thomson (2014) address this issue in depth and in relation to the so-called literature review among several other writing activities. The land is already well-populated with more experienced scholars, rules and debates, alliances, and feuds. Yet, novice scholars are expected to be critical and decide which concepts, debates, and findings to include and exclude. Rather than an adventurous journey, they suggest the metaphor of "occupied territory." It may be dramatic, they state; however, the metaphor "gets closer to the affective experience and intensity of identity work that many doctoral researchers experience" (Kamler & Thomson, 2014, p. 31).

Developing Voice

Traveling the landscape or the occupied territory involves working explicitly with the balancing act of originality and convention. This act is addressed in the term *researcher voice*. Voice is that which allows researchers to write distinctively and increase the possibility that their work is read, because the way the message is conveyed makes it a worthwhile endeavor. Voice is a dialogical phenomenon that can be practiced in apprenticeship-like relations as a part of doctoral learning process (and beyond). There are strong links between voice, the ability to express oneself, and persona or identity, but voice is not to be understood as a matter of finding one's inner self or expressing one's true identity. Rather, we regard voice as part of the researcher writing skills: Voice is a craft that can be practiced, elaborated, and fine-tuned through apprenticeship-like relationships with experienced writers—as in the traditional apprenticeship way of learning a craft from a master. Moreover, such relationships can be found in the most unlikely places and may relate to aspects of being a researcher in a variety of ways: When developing voice, there is a vast world of potential masters to learn from. Becker (1986/2007, p. 33) notes that

> everyone writes as someone, affects a character, adopts a persona who does the talking for them. Literary analysts know that, but seldom examine its implications for academic writing. Academics favor a few classic personae whose traits color academic prose, shape academic arguments, and make the resulting writing process more or less persuasive to various audiences.

Likewise, Elbow, discussing how we learn to write, claims that we "start off singing our own single tiresome pitch for a long time and in that way gradually teach the stiff cells of our bodies to vibrate and be flexible" (Elbow, 1998, p. 282). Elbow's (1998; 2007) discussion of voice contributes to debates on how to understand and teach writing, also at the practical level: How do you learn how to write? We by no means suggest that more voice equals better writing—in many cases this is quite the opposite. In fact, a voice that is too self-conscious risks obscuring the subject matter and purpose of the text. Rather, Elbow's notion of perspective and timing can help the doctoral student ask: What kind of text is it? What do I want to say in this particular piece of writing? Who is my (desired) audience?

Conventions

In all science communities, there are conventions about how to express oneself in order to be recognized and published, and as a member of the science community, these cannot be completely ignored, although they can be and often are pushed, reconstructed, and adjusted over time. These conventions are not only limitations; they also serve a purpose of contentiously constructing and reconstructing the cognitive and social boundaries of a particular discipline or field—demarking what "counts" as scientific knowledge and writing and what does not. In this process, not only doctoral students but also their supervisors, peers, and reviewers play a significant role. Thus, aiming solely for originality would be to neglect the restrictive yet inspirational factors within the research community.

An Experiment of Disarmament

Writing Dialogues

Writing dialogues is one strategy for developing researcher voice and thus allowing originality to evolve. Through three-and-a-half years as part of a doctoral peer writing group, I, Charlotte, had often shared with my peer, Ninna Meier, my enthusiasm over scientists, novelists, and other writers who had inspired us in a diverse range of ways. We had shared our struggle with balancing academic conventions and experimentation while reviewing and discussing our individual manuscripts for papers and dissertation chapters. After finishing our dissertations, we wanted to cowrite and decided to do what we called "an experiment of disarmament." Often mastery is understood as achieving command or performing or grasping something so that there is no longer uncertainty about how it is done or what it involves (Barnacle & Dall'Alba, 2014). Yet, we wanted to balance experiment by disciplined learning from other writers, from our masters, whom we read over and over and whom we admired. What did they actually do that made us admire them so much?

Defensive Writing

Because we had both conducted research in the health care sector, we shared a major interest in the body. We sensed that not only were our empirical data permeated with "bodies" and bodily experiences, the idea of the body was also relevant when we wanted to explore ways of writing about this data. Ellingson (2006) has suggested that the erasure of researchers' bodies from conventional accounts of health research obscures the complexities of knowledge production, resulting in "tidy" accounts. We assumed that these neat pieces might be the result of what Elbow (1989, p. xix) terms "defensive writing": "Defensive writing means not risking: not risking complicated thoughts or language, not risking half-understood ideas, not risking language that has the resonance that comes from being close to the bone." We decided to take the risk of producing untidy texts; however, we might, in addition, create text that lived and breathed.

Thus, we jointly adopted an apprentice state of mind and became co-apprentices learning from each other as well. Elbow (2007) shows how personal writing can remove the focus from a perceived, perfect end result and let the writer experiment and write more freely. To produce the dialogues, we deliberately freed ourselves of any perceived academic audience. We hoped this would allow for more open and less "tidy" texts that tapped into aspects of voice and resonance that drew not only on academic contributions but also on a wider range of sources. In the process of writing we tried to disentangle our academic voice as co-authors from the voices in the letters and to let them speak; not only in their own words but also through the way they speak to each other. These are two of the letters we wrote:

Ninna's Letter

Dear Charlotte,

The book is called *Sorting Things Out: Classification and Its Consequences*, written by Geoffrey Bowker and Susan L. Star. Reading it represented a turning point for me in the process of my PhD: trying to understand how standardization works in health care had caused me much frustration. I remember writing about standardization as an attempt to hold the flexible, stretchable and extremely elastic and volatile fabric of health care work before me with both hands and seeing a pattern in the ways standards and classification systems ran through the fabric as fluorescent threads. But the minute I let go of the material to use my hands to write about it, it would spring back into this convoluted, tightly rolled up yarn of strings in all colors. And I would have to start all over.

Although the topic is both serious and—to some people—seemingly boring, I loved this book and I can never go back to the way things were before I read it. I now snicker at classification systems in the oddest places (how nappy changing stations in public restrooms are often located in women's toilets: apparently only females have babies, males don't—or, if they do, they leave the nappy changing to females?), and I was hooked: hooked on studying standards, classification systems and the entire, "invisible" cognitive, material, and social scaffolding we endlessly draw on, also in my field.

The main thing Bowker and Star taught me was that you can write about seemingly "boring" things in social science and the way you write about the topic can make it interesting, fascinating and eye-opening to others. What a goal to strive towards! One of the ways in which they do this, is that they turn the light on aspects of human experience that we usually take for granted and never pay much attention to, and analyze them with both curiosity and rigor. Doing this, they manage to point my attention to objects and aspects that had escaped my attention and show me how the cognitive and socially "invisible" aspects can hold information and insights that are at the heart of social science.

Bowker and Star use humor and (in some incidents through) unexpected composition of objects and actions to remind us that what we think is "normal" (not reading a phone book as entertainment on a Saturday night) is in fact part of the complex combination of classification systems (phone books are not "real" books to be read for fun or entertainment) that make up the cognitive and social infrastructure we draw on both as people and social scientists. Inspired by their method—shedding light on "invisible" and taken for granted aspects of the practices one study—I attempt to show the relational, situated and dynamically changing aspects of how people think, act and interact in my work.

Charlotte's Letter

Dear Ninna,

I cannot wait. I have to tell you about one of my writing masters right away. I did not remember him until I got your account. What he is doing might be that he makes categories out of elements that do not belong together at first sight or, rather, he makes them belong together by making them vibrate on a shared sounding board. I am not sure, but let's see. His name is Jon-Roar Bjørkvold and he was a professor in music science at Oslo University until 2006. When I wrote my master's thesis in music science (many) years ago, he was my main source of inspiration. There are several reasons for that. The main one is his ontological approach to music, sound and rhythm. His book *The Musical Man* (Bjørkvold, 1989) is not just about music, it is about sound, rhythm and resonance in an essential part of human coexistence. His research deals with the aesthetical dimension of life in a broad sense, the creative urge. In one of the chapters, the vignette "The Triumph of Inconvenience" tells the story of Jon-Roar and his wife relaxing in the deck chairs on the veranda on a sunny summer day. Suddenly they realize that it is actually way too quiet. Panic. Where are the kids? After some searching, it turns out that deep down under the veranda in the humid corner on the rocky ground the kids are having a great time. The triumph of inconvenience. He then tells the story of the five-year-old Per with severe communication problems who sings all day long and almost turns into a butterfly while learning a difficult tune about the splendid butterfly. The chapter also involves Edith Cobb's collection of autobiographies and biographies of creative people (Cobb, 1959) and two preschool children's profane paraphrasing of an innocent singing game (completed with an ink drawing of their visit to the toilet which framed the creative reinterpretation).

Another reason that I rediscover now that I am writing to you about adopting an apprentice state of mind is his reversal of master and apprentice. In a recent interview, he states that regarding children and pedagogies, the children's learning is of paramount interest (Bjørkvold, 1991/2009). What he does, however, is to ask what he can learn from the child. Through studies of child music culture in Norway, Cameroun, The United States, and The Soviet Union, he installs the child as master and himself as apprentice. Distributed masters indeed.

When you feel a bit too comfortable, you need to scare yourself and your reader. When the analysis, the argument, and the whole text are about to become a bit too pearled, too neat, too smug, you must leave the deck chair in the sun and place yourself in the humid, dark corner under the veranda. You must take your time to learn a difficult tune while flapping your arms like a butterfly. You must go to the toilet and paraphrase. You must never consider yourself too grown-up or too academic to continuously keep doing that. And you must do it in writing!

Dismantling Pretentious Scientific Language

The important point here is that we can learn from masters beyond our research field and pay attention to much more than the actual subject of our research. Learning from masters includes paying attention to different forms of expression and ask: Why does this piece of work touch me, entertain me, or bore me? How is this message conveyed? We can decide on decoding the craftsmanship of work we like or admire and try out similar strategies ourselves. While imitating, we decode the craft and as we embrace certain ways of working and expressing ourselves we, eventually, make variations.

Balancing Originality and Convention With Kvale

One way of balancing originality and convention is what we can term the "dismantling of pretentious scientific language." In his article, "The Social Construction of Validity," Kvale (1995) deals with what he terms a "modern legitimation mania." I, Charlotte, read this text while preparing for my oral PhD defense and it felt like a nice uncle patting my cheek and telling me "everything's gonna be OK." How did he manage to do that in writing? In the introduction, he states his aim: "An attempt will be made here to demystify the concept of validity in social research by taking it back to everyday language and interaction" (Kvale, 1995, p. 19). He goes on addressing what he claims to be "the trinity of reliability, validity and generalization" having obtained the status of a scientific holy trinity which appears "to belong to some abstract realms in a sanctuary of science, far removed from the interactions of the everyday world, to be worshipped with respect by all true believers in science" (p. 20). True believers in science. The scene is set for turning upside down ideas of knowledge and belief, science and religion. Then he tells the story of his own encounter with the terms as a young student in Norway trying to memorize these English-Latin terms, which did not belong to the Norwegian vernacular:

> I read heavy texts on the importance of validity, reliability, and generalizability in scientific research. I tried to memorize the definitions of predictive validity, concurrent validity, content validity, and face validity, and I struggled to understand the concept of construct validity. (p. 20)

This introduction is really encouraging and entertaining—a highly recognized social scientist not able to get a grip of core social science terms. This is, of course, not a story of intellectual inability. He is just building his argument from the basis of his own everyday experience to tell a story of how to connect scientific knowledge and everyday experience:

> Later, when traveling in the United States, I learned other meanings of the terms validity and reliability; for example, when cashing a check in the supermarket, I was told that my European driver's license was not valid as identification; when in an academic discussion, I was told that my argument was not valid. Or I heard that the information about the used car I was looking at was not reliable, nor was the car dealer known to be a reliable person. Here the terms valid and reliable belonged to the vernacular, important to the ongoing interactions of everyday life. (Kvale, 1995, p. 20)

Kvale's text is funny because it explodes pretentious scientific language. It is instructive and helpful because it offers an alternative. What we can learn from Kvale's text is to include our own confusion and struggle in writing—not as detached auto-ethnographic illustrations but as a real and relevant part of the epistemological process of knowing. Based on Kvale's personal account and the claim he stakes about academic conventions, we will argue that a researcher is not original just because he or she connects everything, synthesizes, and concludes something never seen before. Originality can be performed through generously sharing epistemological struggle.

Dismantling Pretentious Language

Another master who deals with dismantling pretentious scientific language is Becker (1986/2007). He refers to a former student who agreed with him that certainly she could write shorter and clearer, but she preferred to write as she did because it was *classier*. Taking note of the word *classy*,

Becker elaborates: "None of these classy locutions mean anything different from the simpler word they replace. They work ceremonially, not semantically. Writing in a classy way to sound smart means writing to sound like, maybe even be, a certain kind of person" (Becker, 1986/2007, p. 31).

He sums up, initially about students but then admits that this applies much broader to research:

> They know plain English but don't want to use it to express their hard-earned knowledge. Remember the student who said: "Gee, Howie, if you say it that way it sounds like something anyone could say." If you want to convince yourself that the time and effort spent getting your degree are worth it, that you are changing in some way that will change your way, then you want to look different from everyone else, not the same. (Becker, 1986/2007, p. 41)

The paradox here is that when trying to be different, in the sense of differentiating oneself from lay people through avoiding lay language, we engage in what he terms a "truly crazy cycle" of repeating "the worst stylistic excesses," thus providing "the raw material for another generation to learn bad habits from" (Becker, 1986/2007, p. 41). Knowing the conventions is necessary to be able to travel "occupied territory," and learning from masters is an effective way of decoding the conventions. However, as Becker points out here, some conventions—such as "classy" writing—need to be challenged. In the wording of Picasso, "Learn the rules like a pro, so you can break them like an artist." We need to know the rules and be able to work within the constraints of them in order to choose wisely which ones to break. Otherwise we are just ignorant.

Complying and Adjustment

Research and especially doctoral research is an ever balancing act of complying and adjustment. In an interview study, Brodin (2014) shows that doctoral students experience tensions between critical and creative thinking and note that critical thinking often overshadows creative thinking with the consequence that many students develop a defensive research approach at the expense of an open and independent mind. Creative thinking is often linked to student independency. However, in another publication from the same research project, Brodin and Avery (2014) found that some supervisors expressed their concern about an excessive degree of independence in the students' composition of interdisciplinary research projects combined with insufficient disciplinary knowledge. The authors note that this, in the best case, could lead to original and innovative thinking, while in the worst case it could lead to reinventing the wheel. Thus, both structure and freedom is required and too much independence is not always conducive to doctoral students' creative development.

Encouraging Creative Thinking

Despite this concern, Brodin (2014) concludes that the challenge remains how to encourage doctoral students' creative thinking, since this crucial question is generally missing in doctoral pedagogy. Small creative acts are beneficial for nurturing an open and independent mind as well as knowledge creation and identity formation. Supervisors might thus consider in what ways creative thinking and acting can be encouraged *within* new knowledge development and pragmatic action:

> How can the aspects of making oneself interesting and attaining insight be trained in open-minded and independent directions? Encouraging educational activities of this kind would probably enhance the conditions for students to critically position themselves and foster their self-critical instinct of self-preservation in more constructive directions, which do not primarily aim at avoiding critique or defending oneself. Instead it would strengthen the students' sense of agency and help them to answer perhaps the most universal, intrinsic and fundamental question of every critical and creative scholar: Who am I? (Brodin, 2014, p. 17)

From this point, finding out who we are as researchers is not attained though joining a group of excited people all enthusiastically shouting: "We're all individual." We do not need to claim that each of our papers develop a new concept as John Van Maanen complained at the writing workshop. Rather, we can try out simple models, increasingly moving beyond the original structures and norms.

"Stretching" and "Habits of the Mind"

Several scholars have suggested metaphors to illustrate this creative and disciplined process. For instance, Janesick (2010) uses dance as a metaphor for qualitative research, suggesting "stretching" as a metaphor for the fine-tuning of researcher skills that includes interviewing, observing, narrative, and poetic writing, along with habits of keeping a reflective research journal, the analysis habit, the creative habit, and the collaborative habit, based on Dewey's notion of "habits of the mind" (Janesick, 2010). "Stretching" means exercising the senses and acknowledging subjectivity. Based on Dewey (1910/1997), she argues for developing these habits by "practicing" because "practice" takes time, effort, reflection, and intention, as well as willingness to see the old in new ways and to go beyond preconceptions. Research is thus an ongoing, "open-ended processes of improvisation" (Lave, 1993/2009, p. 204).

Questioning the Research Question

Improvization takes place during all phases of a doctoral research project. To conclude this chapter about tradition and change, we will tell the story of how Charlotte was forced to improvize when her chosen theoretical concepts turned out to collide with experiences in the empirical field. It illustrates that an apprentice approach should not solely apply to learning from and complying with the masters, theories and traditions within the research field. Similarly crucial is an apprenticeship approach to the object of study and the social practices and objects we are studying.

Charlotte's Research Question

The scientific objective of my (Charlotte's) doctoral research was to contribute to the empirical knowledge of employee- and user-driven innovation. By means of intervention studies, the project should contribute to new knowledge about how innovation processes across workplaces and education can be initiated, managed, and especially how new solutions can be integrated across organizations. The project was situated in the social and health care sector involving mini-labs, where professionals from the elderly care sector and professionals from a nursing college were supposed to cross organizational and professional boundaries. The aim was to create new solutions in their shared practices. The theoretical foundation was cross-boundary innovation, as developed and described in Activity Theory (Tuomi-Gröhn & Engeström, 2003). The overall novelty of the project, as anticipated, was that participants across organizational boundaries adopted a shared view and developed shared methods for influence and cooperation. The project should therefore seek out opportunities and barriers to innovation and develop one or more innovative models for collaboration, that is, boundary-crossing innovation. The basic assumption, which I did not question at that time, was that the field was in need of more boundary crossing and that more boundary crossing would lead to more innovation.

The research question was this: How can cross-organizational activities enhance employee-driven innovation in the field of social and health care?

Changing the Plans

But we all live and learn. The start of the project coincided with massive budget cuts in the organizations involved, and when I called my contacts, they all said that their situations were far worse than expected and that right now they were dismissing employees, while the remaining staff was frantically working to accomplish basic tasks. Furthermore, it was a challenge to conduct all the projects that were already underway, and they saw no further space for development. "We have to talk later," they told me, when the chaos was diminished, and they hoped the best for the project. Insidiously realizing that no one in the field was waiting impatiently for a researcher to come and initiate change, in a supervision session with Lene, I decided that I started out with an interview study about actual innovation activities. It turned out, however, that none of the interviewees had stories of innovation through boundary crossing, and most did not see "innovation" as a suitable depiction of the changes in which they were involved. Again, I consulted Lene for more useful and fruitful approaches that could assist me in a more subtle conception of boundary crossing. Lene introduced me to ethnographic fieldwork and shared with me stories about her own experiences as a doctoral field researcher.

Immersed in the Field

I spent months together with intern students, workplace mentors, vocational teachers, managers, and elderly residents. When I observed boundary-crossing activities (e.g., collaborative meetings, cross-organizational projects, and student tutorials to assist their learning across the college and internship at elder care homes) I was not able to observe innovation whatsoever. I read plenty of innovation studies and methodology literature, and I produced two comprehensively written field diaries. I wrote in my reflection log:

Looking for the wrong thing or at the wrong places?

I am reading and writing passionately but I do not have a clue of where this strategy will take me. To be honest, it does not look like or feel like a "strategy" at all. I realize the limitations of my own perspective for understanding the elder care workplaces. The first interview at an elder care center was an eye-opener to my own limited view. I am not at all familiar with elder care institutions as workplaces. The questions in my interview guide about inter-organizational movements and collaboration do not seem relevant, as managers and workplace mentors rarely meet with staff from the college. There is hardly any organizational boundary-crossing that they can tell me about.

Boundary-crossing may be an academic carrot not relevant to most of the people working in the field I am studying. It seems that boundary-crossing is an activity of the few. I may be studying something that does not exist or is not as important as I imagined.

There may be, however, several other boundaries at stake. Mental boundaries between what is possible and what is not, or between what are relevant and irrelevant themes to discuss. The interviewees certainly ask for more organizational boundary-crossing. Are there boundaries that participants want to cross or is it just my own exaggerated fantasies (though informed by theory) of what creates innovation? Could it be that innovation emerges somewhere else? Not at the organizational boundaries?

Dialogue Between Data and Theory

Ongoing sense-making is central in all phases of the research process, from planning of intervention or observation to implementation to processing of data and dissemination of findings or "results." These processes involve the researcher's knowledge of, self-reflection on, and expectation of the field, and no phases are thus unaffected by the researcher's ideas about the nature of the world. However, empirical experiences do not create new insight in itself. What is needed are creative dialogues between empirical situations and theory, and additional innovative theoretical studies (Alvesson & Kärreman, 2011). During the interview study and field observations, my intention became to investigate the premises for my initial theoretical, informed hypothesis, which was that crossing boundaries holds innovation potential. I needed ways to choreograph the dialogue between the data and the anticipated useful theory. I wrote in my dissertation method chapter:

I was driven to explore boundaries in practice, not just other peoples' practices but also to practice boundary crossing myself. Following Dewey (1916), knowing is something which we do. Analysis is behaving towards facts through active experimentation and improvisation. I traced salient situations where intentions for change or change imperatives seemed obvious to me and where actual change occurred in some occasions, while efforts for stability were prevalent at other times. My aim then became to study boundary as a multifaceted concept that may evolve both through focused cross-boundary activities to create change and through everyday work when people interact in situations requiring creativity, intuition and presence. I also sought to study activities that did not fit into my ideas of what boundary crossing might be, and at times during fieldwork, I deliberately "forgot" my theoretical concepts and just immersed myself in the activities that happened to unfold. I observed everyday work at the college and the elder care centers; I observed teaching, caregiving, the mentoring of students. It seemed that boundaries changed, emerged, and disappeared in chaotic patterns. The designated sites were not what I had anticipated as sites of boundary-crossing practices. Flick (2009) observes that research questions usually originate with the researchers' personal biographies and their social contexts. Likewise, Agee (2009) finds that many of her students are "in love" with a particular theory even before shaping their questions, and that their own life experiences have often played a role in their choice of research topic. I was indeed in love with the idea of boundary-crossing between different organizations, mainly because I saw myself as crossing boundaries throughout my life. The study could have concluded that the organizations I had studied were populated by people who did not have capabilities or time for innovation.

A New Research Approach

Continuous dialogue with my supervisor and with peers, reading theory, and writing reflection logs gave rise to a new research approach with a micro perspective on activities, artifacts, and discourse in the local practices and on particular innovative qualities of these activities. The overall research question eventually became this: How do social practices across boundaries unfold in social welfare and health care in the light of innovation imperatives?

This question emerged through a pragmatic understanding of knowledge as the logic of everyday life, where we try to create meaning from what we are experiencing. As researchers, we construct stories about our work, about the world, about ourselves, and about the texts and knowledge we create. Stories are constructed not by individuals on their own but in relation to social practices. The construction and interpretation of the researcher's practice takes place in relation to and through interaction with the supervisor and peers in the scientific community and in dialogue with the researcher's theoretical and empirical fields. Thus, this ongoing practice involves continuing meaning making and construction of knowledge based on knowledge and experiences already present in the field. In Chapter 4 we will further examine the possible tensions between originality and contribution by addressing creativity in the context of doctoral work and supervision.

Good Advice for the PhD Student

- Let go of the ambition to be original.
- Try out strategies for focusing attention and keep an idea bank and reflection log.
- Find peers that you trust and encourage one another to do experimental writing.
- Take the time to learn the rules and find peers with whom you can play or break the rules.
- Note the effects of breaking a rule—does it result in relevant, novel insights or worthwhile writings? Test the effects in dialogue with peers and your supervisor.
- Trust that you will produce original research. In a crowd claiming "We're all individuals," originality may grow from the statement: "I'm not . . ."

Good Advice for the Supervisor

- Introduce the student to the traditions and discussions in the field.
- Introduce the student to research methods and discuss their appropriateness for specific research questions and knowledge aspirations.
- Involve the students in your own choices and experiences with research methods and ways in which they have worked or not worked for you.
- Encourage your students to question their research questions.
- Encourage students to write in different genres and with different purposes. Reflections about research methods, struggles with theoretical concepts, and identity issues are more likely to inform the overall research project when they are processed and kept in writing.

Conclusion

Making an impact is an ambition inherent in the practice of research profession. The outcome of a doctoral research project is supposed to live up to some kind of novelty criterion. In this chapter, we have addressed how novelty aspirations must be balanced with humbleness and involvement in routines and traditions of the field. It is often suggested that we must "jump out of the box" to be original. Making an original contribution is not a seal of quality in itself, and it is certainly not an ambition that serves the newcomer's creativity. Rather, a creative and original contribution can be achieved by selecting and critically using models and knowledge that are already present in the field. We have illustrated and discussed some strategies that have proved to work for ourselves. In general, these strategies serve to enhance experiment, self-reflection, and critical dialogue with others. Grounded and creative research can be achieved by means of habits for fine-tuning research skills. This involves both humbleness and audacity and can be achieved through a strategy that we term "moving on to the edge of the box" instead of jumping out of it.

References

Agee, J. (2009). Developing qualitative research questions: A reflective process. *International Journal of Qualitative Studies in Education, 22*(4), 431–447.

Alvesson, M., & Kärreman, D. (2011). *Qualitative research and theory development: Mystery as method.* Los Angeles: Sage.

Barnacle, R., & Dall'Alba, G. (2014). Beyond skills: Embodying writerly practices through the doctorate. *Studies in Higher Education, 39*(7), 1139–1149.

Becker, H. S. (1986/2007). *Writing for social scientists: How to start and finish your thesis, book, or article* (2nd ed.). London: University of Chicago Press.

Bjørkvold, Jon-Roar (1991/2009). *Den Musiska Människan: Barnet, Sången och Lekfullheten Genom Livets Faser.* [The Musical Man: The Child, The Song and Playfulness Through Life]. Oslo: Freidig Forlag.

Brodin, E. M. (2014). Critical and creative thinking nexus: Learning experiences of doctoral students. *Studies in Higher Education,* ahead-of-print.

Brodin, E. M., & Avery, H. (2014). Conditions for scholarly creativity in interdisciplinary doctoral education through an Aristotelian lens. In E. Shiu (Ed.), *Creativity research: An interdisciplinary and multi-disciplinary research handbook* (pp. 273–294). London: Routledge.

Cobb, E. (1959). The ecology of imagination in childhood. *Daedalus, 88*(3), 537–548.

Dewey, J. (1910/1997). *How We Think.* Dover: Dover Publications.

Dewey, J. (1916). *Democracy and education: An introduction to the philosophy of education.* New York: McMillan.

Elbow, P. (1981). *Writing with power: Techniques for mastering the writing process.* New York: Oxford University Press.

Elbow, P. (1998). *Writing with power: Techniques for mastering the writing process* (2nd ed.). New York: Oxford University Press.

Elbow, P. (2007). Voice in writing again: Embracing contraries. *College English, 70*(2), 168–188.

Ellingson, L. L. (2006). Embodied knowledge: Writing researchers' bodies into qualitative health research. *Qualitative Health Research, 16*(2), 298–310.

Flick, U. (2009). *An introduction to qualitative research* (4th ed.). Thousand Oaks, CA: Sage.

Gioia, D. A. (2006). On Weick: An appreciation. *Organization Studies, 27*(11), 1709.

Janesick, V. J. (2010). *"Stretching" exercises for qualitative researchers* (3rd ed.). Thousand Oaks, CA: Sage.

John-Steiner, V. (1997). *Notebooks of the mind: Explorations of thinking.* Oxford: Oxford University Press.

Kamler, B., & Thomson, P. (2014). *Helping doctoral students write: Pedagogies for supervision.* Oxon: Routledge.

Kroll, J. (2010). Living on the edge: Creative writers in higher education. *TEXT, 14*(1). Retrieved from http://www.textjournal.com.au/april10/kroll.htm.

Kvale, S. (1995). The social construction of validity. *Qualitative Inquiry, 1*(1), 19–40.

Lave, J. (1993/2009). The practice of learning. In K. Illeris (Ed.), *Contemporary theories of learning: Learning theorists in their own words* (pp. 200–208). London and New York: Routledge.

Mills, C. W. (1952/1980). On intellectual craftsmanship (1952). *Society, 17*(2), 63–70.

Pillutla, M. M., & Thau, S. (2013). Organizational sciences' obsession with "that's interesting!" Consequences and an alternative. *Organizational Psychology Review, 3*(2), 187–194.

Tuomi-Gröhn, T. & Engeström, Y. (Eds.). (2003). *Between school and work: New perspectives on transfer and boundary-crossing.* Oxford: Emerald Group Publishing.

Van Maanen, J. (2013). Publication workshop. The Annual University of Liverpool 8th Ethnography Symposium, Liverpool, August 28–30.

Chapter Four
Making the Most of Obstacles

Abstract

Purpose: The purpose of the present chapter is to examine how one can best apply creative processes to PhD work.

Central message: Rather than considering creative processes as more or less self-generated, we argue that resources for creativity must be found in the research landscape.

Takeaways: Creativity grows from repeated routines and practices, but these have come under pressure in various contexts in modern life. The chapter challenges the reader to use "deviation" and experiments to become more creative as a researcher.

Keywords: Creative research, deviation and obstacles, inspiration, everyday life research, stumbling data, absorption and Facebook, Friday detours.

Research as a Creative Endeavor

Most of what I write is inspired by ideas that crop up when doing my morning run—in other words, ideas that come from physical and practical activities. How hard can I push myself? How much rest is the right amount and what is too long a rest period? How long can I run, reasonably speaking, and when am I just being obstinate? How much attention should I pay to my surroundings and how much should I focus on myself? To what extent should I believe in my own abilities and when should I begin to doubt myself? (Murakami, 2008, p. 85).

Most research is, per definition, a creative endeavor. We do research to create new knowledge and/or, new techniques and technologies to ensure the survival and growth of societies and to make peoples' lives better. This is one of the grand and defining narratives of research and science in modern societies. As a researcher, it is troublesome to be short on ideas for new research projects and papers. If research is defined as being creative per se, lacking ideas, not feeling creative, or being unsure about one's own contribution can be a really difficult phase in a research journey. So how do we make the most of obstacles in our lives, and how do we learn to use difficulty as an enabler of production and creativity? What inspires our work? What attracts us to our research subjects? The Japanese writer Haruki Murakami, cited earlier, is running. Here, we will look into creativity resources in today's research landscapes.

How Can I Contribute and Do Creative Research?

In a recent paper, Robert Sternberg (2014), reflecting on his own research career, commented on the fact that he began researching creativity in a period when he was lacking ideas. Later, he began researching love in a period in his life when love was difficult for him. Writing blocks, identity crises, and insecurity can quickly become obstacles when one is unsure how to contribute to one's field. For most doctoral students, the "critical transition" from being a student to becoming a professional is defined by a need to create ideas and stay productive. During this transition, graduate students must make a crucial shift from the familiar realm of course-taker (a consumer of knowledge that is "carefully doled out in the form of courses or modules, course outlines and reading lists, lecture topics and assessment tasks" in tightly bounded and controlled environments) to that of independent scholar (Lovitts, 2005).

How to Apply Creative Processes to PhD Work

Our purpose in this chapter is to examine how best one can apply creative processes to PhD work. We will give a number of examples of others' achievements in this regard. Lovitts (2005) says that people seldom pay attention to PhD students' creative processes or the development thereof, because many tutors believe (mistakenly) that creativity is more or less self-generated. As elsewhere in this book, we would like to challenge this individualistic view of research and show how one can work to bring creative processes into the landscapes of research. We will also argue that creativity grows from repeated routines and practice and that these have come under pressure in various contexts. We will show how one can use "deviation" and experiments in everyday work to become more creative as a researcher. Most especially, our perspective recognizes that there are large resources with a potential for research and that innumerable ideas lurk in one's own and others' day-to-day experience. The question of becoming more creative as a researcher is not a matter of looking elsewhere or pursuing what is new; in fact, creativity can simply be the fruit of examining what is close at hand.

Data on Deviations and Research in Everyday Life

When asked about the circumstances of their creative inspiration, people often cite unexpected places and sometimes surprising environments, such as the daily run or waking in the night with a brilliant idea (Stadil & Tanggaard, 2014). We both have found that good ideas for new research projects can arise in all manner of seemingly unhelpful milieu, such as when drinking coffee with a colleague; going into a random shop and seeing a thought-provoking advertisement; or overhearing a conversation in the bus, cinema, or supermarket. Creativity can come at any place, but it is often prompted when we begin to wonder about phenomena, when we, metaphorically speaking, "stumble onto something," or deviate from a plan.

Examples of the creative process may include a conversation that sticks in our memory, a chance observation made at work or in school, or an advertisement that provokes or causes anger without our immediately being able to say why. When an experience constitutes an example of data, it can be because it seems so strange or awkward that we begin to reflect on and learn from it. Examples of stumbling over data from everyday life are almost endless; this shows that almost any event can provide data (Latour, 2005).

To Stumble and Learn

In the aforementioned sense, it is not bad to stumble. To stumble upon something is to be in a position to find out new things about the world we live in. It is through deviations and noteworthy events that the social world becomes evident or an object to reflect upon. Deviation often fuels the imagination, and this may lead to a break with habitual assumptions about everyday life. "Imagination" is understood here as one of the most important dimensions in the process of turning instances of stumbling into creativity. Imagination allows people and groups to think beyond the given, the here-and-now, and to envisage alternatives, to create parallel worlds, or to travel through time, in the past or in the future. Imagination is both extremely individual—people imagine their unique futures—and deeply social, in its constituents (imagination is fed by media and other kinds of shared representations) (See Zittoun & de Saint-Laurent, 2015).

In order to conceptually understand the creative dimension of stumbling upon something, we will (again) draw on the pragmatist epistemology developed by John Dewey (1938). According to Dewey, most of one's life is based on routine and habit (also known as tacit knowledge); thinking and reflection become necessary only at the point where habitual life cannot continue unchanged. In this sense, imagining what might happen next, or thinking about what has happened, is necessary only when ordinary practices cannot continue unchanged. These instances, or thoughts, which involve imagination, may be seen as an attempt to re-establish balance after an error or to understand the nature of the apparent strangeness in order to be able to take action in response. According to the principles of pragmatism, all knowledge is connected to action, either directly (as in action research) or with respect to the development of "thinking technologies" that enable us to deal with new situations in the future (Brinkmann, 2012a).

How Can We Stumble Creatively?

As mentioned, knowledge is not something mirroring nature, or achieved by passively observing things, but something that arises when there is a disconnection between existing understandings of a phenomenon and the "here-and-now" encounter with the phenomenon we are trying to understand. To take a specific example: One day in the supermarket, you meet a friend whom you have not seen for many years. She says "hello" to you, but you do not immediately recognize her. The friend's appearance has changed; she now dresses in a more grown-up way and her hair is shorter and turning gray. You might find it difficult to recognize her as the "same" as before. As a result, even in only minor ways, you might have to change your assumptions about your friend; accordingly, new knowledge arises within the situation. You now know her as a different person, at least going by her appearance. Meeting her again, you become curious. Has she also changed her political opinions? What about sports and music, which were her favorite topics of conversation years ago? Is she still with her husband, and what about her job situation? In Dewey's sense, you now begin an enquiry, initiated by bumping into your friend by chance.

Relearning the Joy of Experimentation

If you do not stumble on a regular basis, or at least are not aware of this happening, one of the most important things you can do in order for creative deviations to occur is to relearn the joy of experimentation and *learning by doing* or *learning by failing*. A renowned Danish fashion designer, Henrik Vibskov, frequently talks about the importance of "learning through failing." During a TV show quoted in Tanggaard (2014, p. 6), he said, "Failures are my main means of learning." According to Vibskov, mistakes can initiate a creative process because they point toward something that could not be imagined before venturing into the experience. This is the impetus that is familiar to many of us: contact with, or resistance afforded by, the materials with which we work gives rise to new ideas. Creative imagination is fundamentally relational, arising in the space between subjects and objects—even if the immediate experience may be an impression that good ideas pop into our heads seemingly out of nowhere.

Many scientific discoveries are the result of the phenomenon we call stumbling. This approach sees errors as positive. After all, we talk about "coming across" or "stumbling across" a great offer or a good idea. Again, stumbling is a positive thing. To stumble upon things (in this figurative meaning) is a precondition for being able to see the world in interesting ways. It is when stumbling that we can break with the habitus that characterizes most of our everyday lives. To benefit from instances of stumbling upon something, we must be open to the new data we encounter whenever we happen to run into new solutions. To do this, we must keep our "antennae out" and be curious about the world, making the most of obstacles.

Absorption and Deadlines

In many ways, creativity is a core ingredient of research. But is it possible to be creative when one is required to operate under a short deadline and demonstrate efficiency? When even PhD students are now expected to publish their work at the earliest possible opportunity and conclude their studies without delay?

In *Notebooks of the Mind*, Vera John-Steiner (1997) lays down a series of preconditions for creativity. One of these is absorption and deep concentration on the area one is hoping to contribute new ideas to. She has come to this conclusion by studying the biographies of known authors and artists. One such figure is the French physicist Pierre Curie, who together with his wife, Marie Curie, received the Nobel Prize for the discovery of radium. Marie Curie explains in her book on her husband's work: "It seems to me, that already from his early youth, it was necessary for him to concentrate his thought with great intensity upon a certain definite object in order to obtain precise results, and in that it was possible for him to interrupt or modify the course of his reflections to suit exterior circumstances" (p. 47).

Undisturbed Concentration

Deep, constant, and undisturbed concentration was one of Pierre Curie's tools. This is also shown in the writing of Howard Gardner in the 1997 book titled *Extraordinary Minds,* where it is said that Sigmund Freud, the founder of psychoanalysis, often isolated himself in his room and preferred solitude. But what are the conditions for such absorption in a researcher's life today? If we turn our attention to our own research landscapes, we see that it has become harder to be alone. We are asked to be available and preferably work together, in collaboration with other institutions and faculties. E-mails keep flowing in; Facebook demands to be checked; and we may feel the need to update LinkedIn and Twitter, too. There is no shortage of interruptions and offers to join networks, relevant or not. We can access our work e-mails at all times, whether grocery shopping or talking to a good friend we have not seen for some time. Some of us regularly get a kick out of checking news sites, e-mails, and Facebook or posting sometimes casual news about ourselves on various Internet sites. One day, Lene came up against this problem of concentration so frequently that she decided to write about it:

Lene's Constant Distractions

It could be any day whatsoever. I have decided to tackle a new article. The children have gone off to school. I have five hours. At 13.00 hours I must leave for a lecture and workshop I have promised to give to a group of teachers and school leaders about creativity in school. I have turned on the computer. I have made coffee and opened Word, and the cursor sits there flashing. I write a couple of words. I notice that the computer has automatically selected the Calibri font. That annoys me. I would rather write in Times New Roman. I quickly change the font. Write a few more words. Whilst writing, I suddenly think about the clothes in the tumble dryer. Should I perhaps just take them out and fold them? I will be late home and I know that my sons will need their football kit for the afternoon game. It would be better to do the folding now so that it's all ready for the boys. They soon ought to be doing it for themselves, I think. I go down to the cellar to see to it. Fifteen minutes later I am back at the computer. I sit for a while. I think about how hard it is to begin something new. It's much easier to continue working on something that one has already started. The thought enters my head that I must pay the handball club subscription. Take out my iPhone. I often use the notepad function. The older I get and the more I have to do, the harder it is for me to remember things. It's better to make a quick reminder to pay the subscription. It is too bad if you don't pay on time. I also manage to send an e-mail to a colleague about a promised personal development meeting and answer an e-mail from a special student with a question on her section on methods. I catch myself starting to answer the other waiting e-mails. Meanwhile I notice a growing frustration at how I am letting myself be distracted by all these things. Neither the laundry nor the subscription are important right now—they can be done another time. And students often find their own answers if I wait a little before answering. Why can I not discipline myself to write for at least two hours and do the other chores during a break? I make an effort not to look at the vase of faded flowers in the living room and force myself to concentrate on the text. Gathering myself, I begin to write. I decide to write at least a couple of pages and send a draft to my colleague. Meanwhile, I can continue to think about the text, and hopefully my colleague will write back about it. The piece is about the things that promote or hinder creativity. Perhaps it's not just me who is constantly distracted. Perhaps distraction is one of our time's greatest obstacles to creativity?

If we return to the introductory stories about deep concentration—one of the ingredients in the recipe for winning the Nobel Prize—we have to wonder whether Pierre Curie and Sigmund Freud let their minds wander. The two scientists may not have been distracted by Facebook or the laundry or students, but by the leaves on the trees or a longing to walk to a café. We do know that they were good at creating the space in which to concentrate. These days, we have not only leaves in the wind, but also inviting offers to connect on Facebook, not to mention the many hours dedicated to teaching, administration, documentation, and monitoring—all of which are challenges in the life of the researcher. But can such distractions be useful, too? There is something to suggest that this might be the case. Rarely do such associations, or a surrender to the flow of the situation, form the subject of a written record. But here is an example wherein Charlotte, in fact, tries to grasp just such a process of useful disturbances. The reason why it is available in writing is that she and a colleague, Ninna Meier, are investigating which authors inspire their writing processes. They are working on identifying and describing the concept of "voice" in a meeting with their writing tutor. (We will return to strategies of apprenticeship in connection with writing in Chapters 6 and 7.) Here is an example of a productive distraction:

Charlotte's Friday Detour

This morning, I took my time with the Friday newspaper. I am going to work at home today, and I have a long to-do list. This week, I have worked a lot but I have not been able to tick off anything on the list. Yesterday, I submitted an abstract to a call for a special issue about "leisure" in which I argued that the division of work and leisure is unproductive. Leisure behavior at work can enhance both productivity and creativity, I wrote. This is my way, twisting things a bit or staking a cocky claim. So far it has turned out to be a fairly good working strategy for both being invited to write more and for keeping my mind agile. I aim at taking action immediately and not spending much time—just skip it off and see if the idea survives. It seems to be a sound working strategy in many circumstances of research life: do not wait to share until you have finished and polished every thought. If the idea perishes, it does not hurt too much. If the idea lives, then the hard work of questioning, refining, and communicating is about to begin. However, being already involved in dialogue, I have energy from sources other than myself. Ideas may be born in solitude, but they need a community to grow.

The Friday newspaper comes with a Books section, and I always plunge into it immediately. Today there is a double page written by the young Danish novelist Josefine Klougart, in which she tells the story of her rereading of the French writer Marguerite Duras. Her first encounter with Duras 10 years earlier had been determinative for her decision to write and for even getting a sense of what writing means, she says. Listen to what Klougart (2014) tells us about this encounter (translated from Danish):

> Duras introduced me to a voice I could trust, a voice which made me think that literature, first of all, is borne by a voice that you simply believe in. Deceitful and affected, plain and waffling, but always in some way present and consistent, maybe in its discontinuity and or abruptness, always a voice you feel safe about because it has a kind of authority which cannot be ignored. A voice which can do everything—and the things it cannot do—become insignificant to the reader at that moment. We are engaged in the world that this voice gestalts.

What is authority in writing? An authoritative voice can be both deceitful (at least in fiction), affected, plain, and waffling. This is not about finding one's own voice. This is not about expressing identity. An authoritative voice may be one that is present. How does one manage to be present in one's texts? According to Klougart, Duras does it this way:

> The connections between her different scenes exist, but she does not deign a word, sometimes not even an innocent "as." At the same time, this is what shines the most—everything's relatedness. Her focus is so strong, and the scenes stand out so clearly that the connections become obvious and inherent. Things connect from the inside.

Klougart is staying at a writing refuge to do a final editing of her novel before it goes to press, but instead, she finds herself "irreverently" rereading Duras (switching between different novels, reading only parts of chapters) and writing new documents herself. She returns back home with an almost complete manuscript for a new novel. She has not ticked anything off her to-do list, but she has created something new by making Dura's texts shine on her own. What she learned may be that a voice is authoritative not because it connects everything, synthesizes, and concludes; it might be authoritative because it is generous with epistemological struggle and willing to involve with other voices, including the reader's. A voice is authoritative because it is present in the act of getting to know something.

It might be due to a Friday state of mind, but detours are apparently unavoidable today. However, if masters can be found everywhere, we need to be agile "in the moment" to actually see a master when he or she is there. Then we can only tell efficient time from idle time retrospectively.

When We Skip

The above note was written in a rush this actual Friday morning. Reading the newspaper and writing the note did not look like or feel like work. However, new ideas about voice appeared during the process. Theories on incubation (Sawyer, 2012) maintain that the brain continues to work on a problem at the very moment when there is no direct connection to the particular issue. Incubation is used as the term for the subconscious, unguided procedures that are carried out when we are in the throes of addressing an issue or are faced by a challenge. Incubation is often part of the formulation of the "Y" in the abduction process, which provides an understanding of that which is not yet understood ("X"). The most famous example of incubation is the experience of the Greek mathematician Archimedes. Sawyer provides the background in his book *Explaining Creativity*. Archimedes had been asked to solve a problem by his cousin, the King in Syracuse. The king had been given a crown of gold but suspected that it was made of silver covered with a thin layer of gold. Archimedes was told that he may not destroy or cut into the crown. One day in the bathtub it suddenly occurred to him as he lowered himself into the water that gold is heavier than silver and that an object with greater mass moves more water. He was so excited that he ran out into the street shouting "Eureka," which means: "I have found it."

Forced Incubation

Since then researchers have tried to reexamine the phenomenon of incubation but none has come up with a serious answer. Wells (1996) carried out a study in which he interviewed 213 professors. He established that their creative production measured in number of publications positively correlated with a type of forced incubation. These researchers practiced a simple method of working in which they deliberately abandoned their manuscripts when they had writer's block. They explained that it was during these periods that good ideas often came to them. Similar conclusions were reached in the book *In the Shower With Picasso: Sparking Your Creativity and Imagination* (Stadil & Tanggaard, 2014). Here Jørgen Leth, a Danish journalist, author, and Tour de France commentator, explains that he goes on a long walk every morning in order to get into his writing mode. The Danish musician Kenneth Bager takes a bath if he is faced with a particularly difficult challenge. Others sleep, run, take breaks, and look for inspiration in places other than their work. And even if folding the laundry and watering flowers sound less exotic, these diversionary tactics can be transformed into creative breaks that give new energy to work. The main point to note is, however, that systematics or the conscious use of a creative break determines to what extent the break or the distraction becomes a promoter of creativity. After all, one has to return to the manuscript and continue to write at some time before the idea of taking breaks can be shown to promote creativity. Otherwise, they are quite simply breaks.

Systematics surrounding creative breaks also point to something that some creativity researchers, as mentioned before, risk overlooking. It is routine and habit that form the background against which the break, distraction, or alternative activity becomes useful. In contrast, Facebook (whether used by researchers or students during a lesson) is a simple disturbance. Or, expressed in another way, such breaks are meaningful only against the background of a process that is without deviations. So it is important to cultivate the routines and habits that form the background for taking the creative break. In other words, we must be able to construct a systematic procedure. It is furthermore important to cultivate the space in which immersion in a subject can take place. Lene's and Charlotte's everyday experiences with distractions proved to be quite common. The point here is that we can, in fact, find deviations in our own experiences and allow them to afford us access to reflection more generally about the problems of creativity. These examples of incubation also show that experiments in creativity research are themselves inspired by legendary events in Greece; tellingly, the legend has a mundane setting.

Apprenticeships and Quick Learning

We have seen that concentration is a central component of creativity; while distractions, with a little luck, can develop into creative breaks. But what is it that creates the conditions for concentration and sustainable work? A very simple question might be: "Where and how can one learn to engage in sustained study as a doctoral student and generally as a researcher?"

A "Fast-Food" Mentality

In Vera John-Steiner's *Notebooks of the Mind,* which investigates creativity, an entire chapter is given over to attempting an answer on this issue. The chapter gives the example of Pierre Curie, and with respect to conditions for concentration, John-Steiner says: "Such a focused attention, necessary for outstanding scientific work, has rarely been encouraged in the context of a class-room" (1997, p. 47). Classrooms are filled with breaks, the coming and going of considerable numbers of people, and changes between classes. People who like to concentrate may thus find it hard to work in a classroom. John-Steiner writes that various authors, artists, and researchers remain strangely quiet when reminiscing about their school life and the classroom; on the other hand, they often talk about the value of a more personal education, which in many ways resembles apprenticeship (see also Lave, 2011).

Today, the classroom is more than ever filled with people and interruptions. Yes, we live in times where a "fast-food" mentality is encouraged, and this even extends to methods of fast learning rather than the traditional apprenticeship. Again, we may apply some data on deviation. In the faculty of psychology at Aalborg University, students are regularly asked to evaluate the teaching. Often taking the form of a customer satisfaction survey, the results can make for quite interesting reading. It's not unusual for students to complain about long lectures. As one of them comments: "I do not comprehend how experts in teaching theory manage to lecture for two hours at a stretch when research has shown that our concentration is limited to 20 minute periods." The student did not manage to provide the reference to the research in question; but the 20-minute rule does seem to have become an accepted fact. We can reflect on this by linking it with data on deviation. In connection with the preparation for a conference workshop, Lene was sent guidance on how to create so-called activating workshops. This contained the following sentences: "If your message is to have any impact on the everyday life of participants as well as their work, it is important that you formulate it in a brief and precise way. Choose between two and four points that can be demonstrated on one or two slides. Ensure that this covers a maximum of 15 to 20 minutes." It is possibly correct that we now find it difficult to concentrate for more than 20 minutes at a time; but are we sure that content is of value for participants' lives only if it comes in packages of less than 20 minutes? It is as if an unchallenged ideology of the quick fix has come to mean that what is delivered quickly is good, and what is slow should be disregarded. Speed equals power.

Creativity Cannot Be Hurried

Numerous researchers have, however, concluded and documented the fact that creativity cannot be hurried. Teresa Amabile (1996) discusses this issue in connection with her research into the relationship between motivation and creativity. Various courses that offer a quick fix are seldom as effective in boosting creativity as simply being preoccupied with something—for its own sake. Deadlines or slight pressure can indeed make us up the pace and work harder; but where there is constant pressure, felt as an external controlling force, this hinders creativity. John-Steiner (1997) cites the French photographer Henri Cartier-Bresson: "The potential of every human of becoming an artist remains unfulfilled without the individual's acquaintanceship and immersion into the artistic traditions of the past, and the distinctiveness of his culture." John-Steiner further illustrates this question with an example relating to Mozart and apprenticeship: "It is known that the elder Mozart devoted himself totally to his son's musical education, and the father's expectations were enormous" (p. 40). A master can be either a parent, teacher, or another devoted person; here, no one talks of the quick fix. Thus, John-Steiner concludes: "Intellectual and artistic development is slow and it does not take place as a straight and continuous process" (p. 51).

Craftsman

Similarly, Sennett writes in *The Craftsman* in 2010 about apprenticeship as the way to achieve good results in a piece of work. For the same reason, he is not enthusiastic about creativity, which he relates to a romantic and idealistic research tradition wherein the values of hard work, practice, routines, and tradition are often ignored in favor of a preoccupation with imagination and what is novel (innovation) or easy. Yet no one is saying that the concept of creativity must always be linked to such traditions, especially if they hinder people's opportunities for creativity. We have advocated in several books and articles the value of apprenticeship for creativity—for example, in connection with the fact that you can identify the new if you know about the old: it is easier to improvise if you know the score. Several descriptions of the lives of creative people (by which is meant people who have contributed works and meaningful production to their environments) identify apprenticeship as a vital ingredient (Gardner, 1997; John-Steiner, 1997; Hasse, 2001; Sennett, 2010; Tanggaard, 2008; Tanggaard & Brinkmann, 2009). And apprenticeship is by definition a long-term thing. According to Sennett (2008), it takes 10 years to become good at something and another five years to arrive at the moment where you can help to contribute something new and creative to a given field. Andreas Golder, a Russian-born artist living in Germany, tells in the book *In the Shower With Picasso* (2014) that it took him nine years to learn to paint like the old masters, from which point he began to develop his own style. Creating something new can often involve the re-creation and reworking of the old. Jørgen Leth explains that he makes a virtue out of this by working with "ready-mades," using his own text, material, or scenes from existing films. Only those well-versed in art and text discern this play with existing material; generally a thorough knowledge of what has gone before is required. Perhaps it is creative to experiment with passages in one's lectures and writings when teaching. But it is doubtful to what extent this promotes creativity in the audience.

The McDonaldization of Research

Our last example comes from the day-to-day work of a researcher. We are both concerned with qualitative research and read many research articles referring to a qualitative approach. Lately we have been struck by the standardization apparent in many articles. As mentioned above, much of today's research appears to be performed under a feeling of obligation: there is significant pressure on researchers to publish. It is therefore becoming harder to spend years completely immersing oneself in new and undefined areas that are perceived as risky, even if it is here that the most significant breakthroughs can be made. This tendency can be seen in most research disciplines, since funds for free research are dwindling; most funds are channeled through pools that are subject to the political interests of the day. It can be nearly impossible to obtain financing for research that does not lead directly to practice. Even if the research does obtain funding, this can appear to be a waste of energy if it fails to yield dividends in the form of (copious) publications. Instead, there is a tendency to play it safe and use well-known and tested models. We would apply the label "McDonaldization" of research to this development, which we believe is a threat to creativity.

The sociologist George Ritzer (2008) has been particularly preoccupied with the concept of the McDonaldization of society in a way that has inspired others to analyze more specific fields in the light of this metaphor. Nancarrow, Vir, and Barker (2005) thus analyzed qualitative market research as a McDonaldizing practice, and Brinkmann (2012b) expanded the perspective to apply to qualitative research as such. Here we will outline four aspects of McDonaldization and show how it risks suppressing the opportunity for exciting and creative research. Our focus is primarily on qualitative research in the human and social science disciplines, since this area is most familiar to us from our work. However, we assume that similar analyses could be made for other types of research.

Efficiency

Efficiency is the first aspect of McDonaldization. This is a matter of choosing the quickest and most economic path from A to B. Today, the talk is of LEAN and optimization. Within the research world, there is widespread discussion of *methods* that promote efficiency. The word *method* comes from the Greek language and originally meant "the path to a goal." But a one-sided focus on method alone leads to an excessive concern, with the need to avoid iteration, slowness, or flexibility with respect to the premises in one's field because one believes that only by following a method can a swift and efficient result be guaranteed. Thorough, creative research, of course, requires time and patience. Sometimes it is necessary to reject existing methods and develop others, or work more freely with a variety of methods. Among other things, methods are developed with the aim of minimizing time spent—so that you don't have to reinvent the wheel every time—but in fact, it is impossible to be properly immersed in a subject if everything in the research process has to be geared to the minimal use of time and resources. Fieldwork—which is difficult to characterize as a method, since it is a life practice and type of investigation—can, for example, take months or years. We suspect that the qualitative research interview has become the most widespread method in that field today, not just because it is an important method, which it is, but also because it offers a quick and efficient means of obtaining data. Unfortunately, it is sometimes forgotten that not all questions can be answered using this method; certainly some questions do not lend themselves to this type of "snapshot" approach, which is the way of much research conducted by interview. A mere 60 minutes might be spent on each research participant before moving on. This is a type of qualitative tourism: it cannot provide insight or the type of results achieved through in-depth study.

Calculability

Calculability is the next aspect. Calculability is part of "New Public Management'" and its attendant culture of documentation, evidence-based practice, and evaluation. Everything must be calculated and determined on the basis of clear objectives laid down in advance. This is apparent in qualitative research, with project descriptions prescribing interview requirements such as "40 interviewees, 20 men and 20 women." It is often left unexplained why precisely 40 (and not four, or 400) should be the relevant number. There seems to be an attempt to imitate an ideal concept of calculated rationality. This does not suit the emergent, processual character of qualitative research.

Predictability

Predictability is the third aspect. This has to do with uniformity across contexts, among other things. At McDonald's, you have to know what a Big Mac is and how quickly it can be produced, irrespective of your location in Beijing or Baltimore. The basic thought is "Avoid surprises!", but this is contrary to the raison d'être of research, which after all *seeks* the surprising (which we have earlier described as the "breakdown"). Many guides and manuals published over recent years contribute to the drive for predictability by dictating the approach, irrespective of the population and subject being investigated.

Control

Control is the final aspect of McDonaldization and is discussed by Ritzer (2008). Control is about de-skilling—that is, one removes skills from people from the point of view of control, for example by allocating or externalizing skills to technologies (which, naturally, are intended to optimize, streamline, and standardize). Within our branch of research, this happens typically by means of CAQDAS—computer-assisted qualitative data analysis software. It is not uncommon for a research article to cite a computer program as a method of analysis in its own right. We believe this is extremely detrimental to creativity in research: The creative abduction process cannot be carried out by a computer program. There is nothing wrong with the software itself; but if one believes that it can replace a thorough, intensive, patient, and creative reading of the material, then one is mistaken. Furthermore, programs are primarily developed for coding, as for example practiced within Grounded Theory; they are less suited to other forms of reading and analysis.

Quality and Quantity

Nancarrow et al. (2005) come to the following rather depressing conclusion with respect to the recent McDonaldization of research:

> Just as McWorld creates "a common world taste around common" logos, advertising slogans, stars, songs, brand names, jingles, and trademarks" [. . .], the qualitative research world also seems to be moving towards a common world taste for an instantly recognisable and acceptable research method that can be deployed fast. (Nancarrow et al., 2005, p. 297).

Irrespective of what one might think about McDonald's and the streamlining and standardization that "McDonaldization" expresses, it can hardly be called creative if a researcher simply follows a universal direction. The unfortunate thing is that it is not only researchers who are lemmings running in the same direction, using sensible arguments; preprogrammed systems and incitement structures invite such behavior. Paradoxically enough, these systems and structures have been designed to increase the quantity of research *and* improve its quality (world-class research, more Nobel Prizes, etc.). Yet the opposite effect will most likely result, going by what we know about creativity research. According to the most recent Danish Nobel prize winner, Jens C. Skou, the way in which subsidies and reward systems function in today's research world would have stopped him from doing the creative research in chemistry that led to the award. Another Nobel Prize winner, the physicist Ben Mottelson, also had this to say to the Danish paper *Information*: "If H. C. Ørsted, who discovered electromagnetism in 1820, had lived at the time of the strategic research council, he would instead have been responsible for an improvement in paraffin wax candles"

(Sterling, 2008). The new departure in research in the direction of creativity, whether we are talking about the most empirical natural sciences or the qualitative human and social sciences, requires time, patience, knowledge, courage, and the freedom to linger. These are all factors that run counter to the McDonaldization philosophy, as we have shown.

The counterpoint to McDonaldization of research is, as we wish to emphasize here, to see research as a craft. As previously mentioned, Mills's (1959) classical work on social research spoke of the "intellectual craft," for which no manuals or standardized procedures can be laid down. Instead, the researcher is a type of learn-as-you-go worker creatively forging research with the materials he or she has at hand (empirical analysis, life experience, theoretical concepts, etc.). Every researcher must, like every craftsman, develop their own personal style; not much is said about this in today's books on methods.

Good Advice for the PhD Student

- Accept that getting to know something can be a long and arduous process, and look out for strategies to enjoy it!
- Try to deviate, or "stumble across" things more and be aware of the deviations that you have already made.
- Use your experience and strive to develop your own style as a researcher.
- Seek immersion and surround yourself with things and materials that inspire you.
- Ensure you have space in which to work.
- Accept the tediousness of research work and move forward as and when you can.

Good Advice for the Supervisor

- Learn from your experiences and do not believe that your students can appropriate this knowledge entirely.
- Consider carefully which research experiences can be useful for students.
- Take your students with you into the research workshop to show them what it means to be a researcher.
- Think about how you can guide your students, not only in research methods but also in the way of life of a researcher.
- Lead by example and show how you yourself have learned from your mistakes.
- Give examples of good practice that can inspire your students.

Conclusion

In this chapter we have sought to investigate the conditions of creativity in today's research landscapes. It has been our aim to examine our own everyday experiences to find answers to the creativity challenges that many agree face us today. Creativity is no longer a luxury for the few; but how can we make more people creative? If we proceed from our own experience, it is pressure of time, problems in being allowed to linger on something for a certain amount of time, and the McDonaldization of life and research that emerge as the main barriers to creativity. In investigating this, we examined other researchers' ideas and found that the counterparts of the above barriers were a quiet environment, the inversion of diversionary tactics into useful creative breaks, apprenticeship, and craftsmanship. Some may say there is nothing new here, since these are tried and tested techniques, thousands of years old. Nonetheless, we maintain that they are new, and in any event it is valuable to keep in mind that routines, habits, stability, systematics, and continuity are the background against which new things can grow. Creativity requires openness toward the unexpected and the spontaneous; it is very rare to find room for these elements in our strictly controlled and pressurized modern world.

References

Amabile, T. M. (1996). *Creativity in context*. Boulder, CO: Westview.

Brinkmann, S. (2012a). *Qualitative inquiry in everyday life: Working with everyday life materials*. London: Sage.

Brinkmann, S. (2012b). *Qualitative research between craftsmanship and McDonaldization*. A keynote address from the 17th Qualitative Health Research Conference. *Qualitative Studies, 3*(1), 56–68.

Dewey, J. (1938). *Logic: The theory of inquiry*. New York: Henry Holt & Co.

Gardner, H. (1997). *Extraordinary minds*. London: Basic Books.

Hasse, C. (2001). Institutional creativity: The relational zone of proximal development. *Culture & Psychology, 7*(2), 199–221.

John-Steiner, V. (1997). *Notebooks of the mind*. Oxford: Oxford University Press.

Klougart, J. (2014, July 4). Sommeren 2010 var et rod [The summer of 2010 was a mess]. *Weekendavisen* [Weekend Newspaper; Books sec.], pp. 8–9.

Latour, B. (2005). *Reassembling the social: An introduction to actor-network-theory*. Oxford: Oxford University Press.

Lave, J. (2011). *Apprenticeship in critical ethnographic practice*. Chicago and London: The University of Chicago Press.

Lovitts, B. E. (2005). Being a good course-taker is not enough: A theoretical perspective on the transition to independent research. *Studies in Higher Education, 30*(2), 137–154.

Mills, C. W. (1959). *The sociological imagination* (Denne udgave 2000). Oxford: Oxford University Press.

Murakami, H. (2008). *What I talk about when I talk about running*. New York: Vintage.

Nancarrow, C., Vir, J., & Barker, A. (2005). Ritzer's McDonaldization and applied qualitative marketing research. *Qualitative Market Research, 8,* 296–311.

Ritzer, G. (2008). *The McDonaldization of society* (5th ed.). Thousand Oaks, CA: Pine Forge.

Sawyer, K. R. (2012). *Explaining creativity: The science of human innovation* (2nd ed.). New York: Oxford University Press.

Sennett, R. (2008). *The Craftsman*. New Haven: Yale University Press.

Sennett, R. (2010). *The craftsman*. England: The Penguin Group. Allen Lane.

Stadil, C., & Tanggaard, L. (2014). *In the shower with Picasso: Sparking your creativity and imagination*. London: LIU Publishing.

Sterling, K. (2008, January 4). Nobelprismodtager: Dansk grundforskning i alvorlige problemer [Nobel laureate: Danish basic research into serious problems]. *Information*. Retrieved from http://www.information.dk/152656.

Sternberg, R. J. (2014). I study what I stink at: Lessons learned from a career in psychology. *Annual Review of Psychology, 65,* 1–16.

Tanggaard, L. (2008). *Kreativitet skal læres—når talent bliver til innovation*. Aalborg: Aalborg Universitetsforlag.

Tanggaard, L. (2014). *Fooling around: Creative learning pathways*. Charlotte, NC: Information Age Publishers.

Tanggaard, L., & Brinkmann, S. (2009). *Kreativitetsfremmende læringsmiljøer*. Frederikshavn: Forlaget Dafolo.

Wells, D. H. (1996). Forced incubation. *Creativity Research Journal, 9*(4), 407–409.

Zittoun, T., & de Saint-Laurent, C. (2015). Life-creativity: Imagining one's life. In V. P. Glăveanu, A. Gillespie, & J. Valsiner (Eds.), *Rethinking creativity: Contributions from cultural psychology* (pp. 58–75). Hove and New York: Routledge.

Chapter Five

Peers and Masters Are Everywhere

Abstract

Purpose: The purpose of the present chapter is to discuss the diverse range of learning resources beyond the formal supervisory relationship.

Central message: Strategies for writing are essential throughout the doctoral journey as a means for both learning and production. A distributed notion of apprenticeship allows for a variety of inspirational writing sources.

Takeaways: Writing is the main activity for passing on and exchanging ideas in the research community. Additionally, writing is itself a kind of data collection and a method of inquiry that must be practiced and elaborated throughout the research journey.

Keywords: Writing, researcher identity, writing groups, emotions, experience, sharing, knowledge brokering, a safe training environment, generosity, intuition, private life, epistemological struggle.

Distributed Masters

While the traditional notion of apprenticeship in doctoral training focuses on the relationship between the novice and an experienced master, a distributed notion acknowledges the diverse range of learning resources beyond the formal supervisory relationship. A distributed perspective carries the following encouraging message: Masters are available everywhere for us to seek out, if only we adapt an apprentice-like state of mind. Obviously, this applies to doctoral writing, which is also the main focus of this chapter, but more importantly, we regard an apprentice-like state of mind as one of the most vital attitudes in academia. This state of mind keeps us alert and curious and avoids complacency and mental stagnation.

Given the premise of this book, it is evident that writing is not a matter of truth claims or expressing one's true self. Rather, we suggest that writing is at the heart of thinking and a craft that can be practiced, elaborated, and fine-tuned through apprenticeship-like relationships. In an apprentice relationship, you are not told what to do. Neither are you supposed to just do it your own way or even to be *original*. Often, you are supposed to imitate what the master has done and simply do that for a shorter or longer period of time before you eventually adjust or start experimenting. In our view, a master–apprentice relationship need not be a direct interaction between two human beings. Learning from a master could be understood as learning through written text, a piece of art, and even through everyday life itself.

Apprenticeship Writing

Apprenticeship writing can be performed in relation to more experienced researchers and in peer groups, but there is a vast world of potential masters to learn writing from—in fiction and journalism (Meier & Wegener, forthcoming), through non-linguistic genres of expression such as rock or jazz music (Barley, 2006; Weick, 1998), and via the visual arts (Pink, 2007; Pink, Hubbard, O'Neill, & Radley, 2010). In this chapter, we will look at the peer and master relationship in the broadest terms and explore ways of seeking out masters, learning from them and, equally important, how to be masters ourselves.

Fear and Anxiety

From this perspective, it is discouraging that many studies of doctoral writing and dissertation completion address a variety of problems in the process of writing, which are framed in terms of supervisory absence and loneliness, among others (Jazvac-Martek, Chen, & McAlpine, 2011). A report from an interview study on doctoral student writing notes that "regardless of publication success or failure, the whole process was one of tremendous effort and struggle" (Kamler, 2008, p. 290), and Lee and Boud (2003) identify scholarly writing as an activity involving fear and anxiety, as well as desire. Our own experiences as supervisor and peer confirm that for many doctoral students, the process of writing involves not only anxiety but also an occasional total lack of confidence in one's own ability to express thoughts, and maybe even one's ability to think (anything at all—besides from how to escape academia). In a state like this, it is obviously difficult to get anything written. Statistics illustrate this harsh fact in numbers as mentioned in the Preface. It comes as no surprise that completing the doctoral dissertation is difficult: after all, writing is about transferring observations, ideas, and thoughts into clear, well-structured arguments and lines of reasoning. But that's not all: As novice scholarly writers, doctoral students have much more on the line. Their writing is the main point of assessment of their potential and qualifications, and writer's block is probably one of the most feared conditions among doctoral students. Through their writing, doctoral students need to convince their peers, supervisors, and reviewers of journals that they are indeed highly qualified academics. Their future in academia depends upon it. All of this is to suggest that scholarly writing and identity formation are interwoven, rendering the student even more vulnerable through the process of learning how to write (Wegener, Meier, & Ingerslev, 2014). Thus, writing is not only a cognitive process of information processing (an epistemological process) but more fundamentally an ontological process, an essential part of becoming somebody, an identity-constitutional process (Packer & Goicoechea, 2000).

Supporting a Peer-Review Culture

Writing well entails decoding academic writing conventions as well as becoming a critical, creative researcher (Wegener & Tanggaard, 2013). However, there is currently little inquiry into the everyday events and routines that take place during the doctoral period, and conversations about writing have inevitably favored product rather than process (Colyar, 2009). Across the literature, there is a call for more research into the specific experiences of doctoral students (Jazvac-Martek et al., 2011), studies exploring the network and relationships that influence students' researcher identity (Baker & Lattuca, 2010), and in general more publications from doctoral students' own perspective (Lassig, Dillon, & Diezmann, 2013; D. Maher et al., 2008). Given the peer-review culture of academia, it seems highly relevant that doctoral students should be encouraged to become involved in dialogues on their writing-in-progress, to engage in peer learning (e.g., writing groups), and to explore different apprenticeship strategies.

Writing and Identity Formation in Peer Groups

In their study of factors influencing the successful submission of PhD theses, Wright and Cochrane (2000) point to the necessity of taking into account the psychological and emotional processes that accompany the experience of learning. Academic writing concerns knowledge production and dissemination, yet these processes are closely tied to identity formation. In order to write and publish research, the budding scholar needs to find his or her angle and voice(s) in order to convey the research to an academic audience and/or professional domain. It is a question of how and where to make a contribution.

Much research into writing in higher education has taken undergraduate work as its subject, although doctoral writers are attracting increasing attention (Fergie, Beeke, McKenna, & Creme, 2011). As Badley (2009) has suggested, the lack of focus on doctoral writing in research and curricula may be explained by the assumption that doctoral students do not need to address writing development explicitly. That said, there is a vast range of how-to manuals aimed at doctoral writers themselves, as Kamler and Thomson (2008) note, and add that many supervisors are unaware that their students consult advice books. Yet, when we move through the writerly landscape, everyone has to find their own pathway, the way that is most useful to each of us depending on where we are in the writing process and the purpose of our writing.

Writing Throughout the Journey

Most important, doctoral students must be encouraged to seek out and develop writing strategies from the outset. "I write in order to learn something that I did not know before I wrote it," as aptly noted by one of our own writing masters, Laurel Richardson (2003, p. 501), and this statement also applies to this chapter. Writing is itself a kind of data collection, or a method of inquiry (Richardson, 2003). Several books on writing advise doctoral students how to produce and finish their dissertations. Many students, however, do not read this kind of advice and even if they do, they do not follow it (Becker, 1986/2007). Even worse, if they actually try to follow the advice, they end up feeling confused or inadequate when this seemingly simple advice turns out to be difficult to follow (Walker & Thomson, 2010). This may be because advice books as a genre reduce dissertation writing to a series of linear steps (Kamler & Thomson, 2008). Academic writing is complex, identity-related work, and it is not enough merely to offer a set of tips and tricks to increase output in narrow and short-term ways (Kamler, 2008). As indicated above, we view doctoral writing as a form of discipline-specific social interaction embedded in institutions and social structures. Let's take a closer look at the learning resources of these social and institutional landscapes.

Networks

What seems to be the most important factor in successful completion of the doctorate is the role of students' networks (D. Maher et al., 2008; M. Maher, Fallucca, & Mulhern Halasz, 2013). According to Devenish et al. (2009), the key factor seems to be an ethic of care and pedagogies that emphasize relational rather than regulatory practices. Though these requirements can be met through both supervisor–student interactions and in formal doctoral programs, peer learning and peer support are seen as having particular advantages. There are increasing calls for knowledge creation to be collaborative, and Jazvac-Martek et al. (2011) note that doctoral students' academic futures depend on their ability to extend and maintain a network of relationships. McAlpine, Paulson, Gonsalves, and Jazvac-Martek (2012) point to the fact that students who completed their theses were able to operate independently but sought the emotional support of others, whereas those who did not complete had difficulties in seeking support. Doctoral learning, however, is often an individual rather than a group undertaking, and students' isolation is a frequent problem (Nordentoft, Thomsen, & Wichmann-Hansen, 2012).

Student agency in contexts outside supervision has been discussed, but it has rarely been the explicit focus of empirical or theoretical attention (Hopwood, 2010; McAlpine & Amundsen, 2007). One exception is Lockheart (2010), who describes how team synergies evolved within a PhD writing group of four scholars from different departments. The participants gained confidence and enhanced their ability to write while occupying the roles of writers, editors, and critics. Similarly, Lee and Boud (2003) cite the impact of group pedagogies on developing effective publication strategies, describing how peer groups became rich sites for doing research development work and fostering publications. In a study of peer groups, Aitchison and Lee (2006) found that peer writing groups explicitly tackled questions of knowledge, textual practice, and identity, while Malfroy (2005) found that the power of collaborative knowledge-sharing environments is often overlooked, although collaborative practices enhance students' research capacity.

Writing Groups

Recently, there has been a growing interest in writing groups. This interest represents a distributed notion of doctoral writing and thus a shift from a "vertical" (supervisor–student) framework of peer review to a "horizontal" (student–student) frame (Aitchison & Lee, 2006, 2010; Lee & Boud, 2003).

The mutual giving and receiving of feedback that takes place among doctoral students reading each other's texts transforms the notion of the peer review from a student–expert binary relationship into a democratic and mutual pedagogy (Boud & Lee, 2005). This is not to suggest that we can eliminate the important learning to be derived from supervision. Rather, it is to draw attention to and further recognize the kind of support and learning that can be achieved in peer writing groups. Academic identity is shaped by participatory practices as individuals actively construct identities through interacting with their social contexts (Lassig et al., 2013). Peer groups provide pedagogical space for students to experiment with structural, grammatical, and rhetorical strategies for representing the field they are researching while also trying out various roles as commentators. This experimentation includes "what it looks like and feels like to offer a critique, make a claim, exert an authoritative stance, advance an argument, reflect, position oneself in a text or a field, assert a voice" (Aitchison & Lee, 2006, p. 273). Thus, even though the doctoral group will examine one text at a time, knowledge building and identity formation take place for all members of the group.

Mutuality, Expertise, and Writer Identity

In the next sections, we report from a session in Charlotte's peer writing group, drawing on three concepts proposed by Aitchison and Lee (2006): mutuality, expertise, and writer identity (further elaborated in Wegener, Meier, & Ingerslev, 2014). *Mutuality* refers to the delicate dynamics between power and difference at all levels of group functioning, from the negotiation of groups norms through to the micro-dynamics of turn-taking within specific group interactions. *Expertise* or know-how that advances learning in the peer group comes in multiple forms, depending on the type of group and the needs of its members. Thus, each peer group builds a shared repertoire of language and skills for analyzing and describing texts. Finally, the element of *writer identity* in peer learning refers to questions of voice, authority, and writer positioning, issues that invariably arise in writing groups over time and in relation to the research community the student is about to enter. Through providing this example of a peer process, we aim to *show* the lessons learned, and not *tell* through any recipe or general rules about which steps to follow.

Scene From a Peer Writing Group

The session took place approximately two years after they had initiated this peer group, and the dialogue reveals a somewhat free and direct tone, which may sound stark in this context. However, it is precisely the development of mutual trust that enables this kind of tone to be used freely.

The dialogue opens up for doubt and desire to exist in relation to the actual text being reviewed, as well as wider issues of researcher identity. Charlotte (CW), whose writing is on the agenda that day, is conducting an ethnographic field study of innovation in elderly care, and she has half a year left to submit her thesis. Karen (KI) is also in the dissertation writing process, monitoring an innovation project in a large public hospital. Ninna (NM) has recently passed her oral defense with a comparative case study on health care leadership and management and now brings articles in progress to the group sessions. As preparation for the workshop, Ninna and Karen have received a draft of a chapter for Charlotte's dissertation in which she reviews the literature on innovation, and they have prepared feedback. As we will show here, the writer's needs emerge and are articulated in the session, and ideas are abandoned or elaborated in dialogue, as all three participants exchange their knowledge, experiences, doubts, and desires.

A Neat Literature Review

The initial comment from Charlotte addresses her anticipation about the product she is supposed to create, namely a "neat" literature review for her thesis. She also addresses her lack of control over the writing process:

> CW: What happens is that I start trying to write this neat literature review. I don't know why I can't control it. I feel that it's time for closure. I must write to show that I have read the innovation literature and that I know which of it is relevant in my case. Then I cut out sections from documents that I have written in different phases and think, "I want this part in the chapter, and this part, and this part." And then it ends up as a collage. I gradually lose control. What I initially wanted was to disguise myself and soberly present a state-of-the-art description. However, I find myself deconstructing innovation, and then it ends up as something . . . well, I don't know what it is.

Here, Charlotte expresses an envisioned ideal of an objective writing style in which the writer is invisible, but she also expresses concern about her loss of control over her writing and the direction the text is taking.

Sharing Experience and Know-How

Ninna responds with ideas about the structure of the text, sharing her experience and know-how:

> NM: As I see it, there are two sections. The first part is a sober review of the literature, and that part is a prerequisite for the second part, which tells us what you actually did: "I went into the field to find innovation and this is what

happened." The first is not about how you deal with innovation. It is about the complexity and ambiguity of the concept. And you can show this through the refective process in your writing. I think this is the way to make this chapter a great read and very relevant. I feel that you share Karen's frustration with the innovation concept.

Ninna offers mutuality by referring to some of the same problems that Karen has talked about during an earlier session. Thus, the problem of loss of voice is not individualized but, on the contrary, brought into a shared space of investigation. Ninna advises Charlotte to use her personal frustration as an analytical point of departure.

Questions of Writer Identity

Karen, however, moves to the meta-level and addresses questions of writer identity:

> KI: I think it's important to keep the dialogue at this particular level of abstraction if we are to help you. Maybe you are a deconstructionist? You have a talent for it, at least. I mean, we should be careful not to push you to write a forced "traditional" literature review if you meant it to be something else. You can write a theory chapter, which is a deconstruction, and then you can find a community in which you will be acknowledged, I'm sure. In other communities you would take a serious beating.

Here Karen supports Charlotte's initial desire to carry out deconstruction and transforms it into a question of writer identity by suggesting that she might *be* a deconstructionist. Karen points to the fact that writing conventions are also a matter of choosing the right audience, of finding a scholarly community in which a specific writing style will be acknowledged.

Including Yourself in the Text

Ninna latches on to this point and addresses Charlotte's fear of losing control. Furthermore, she exercises mutuality. She offers her know-how from a position where she simultaneously shows that she has a genuine desire to acquire the skill that Charlotte has: including herself in her texts.

> NM: I think Karen has a point. At this stage it is important to enter a calm state of mind: you need to feel the ice in your stomach! Own the work! Stop writing as the researcher you are expected to be, but realize who you really are. You write well. It is great fun! This is what I personally really want to

practice: to put myself out there in my texts. I don't think you should retreat from the text. Of course, the text needs structure, but when we review Karen's and my texts, we always discuss how to make them more transparent, how to reveal ourselves more. You are actually present in the text, and you are writing transparently. This is both a methodological and a writing tool, because you show that research is a social practice. When you write about your struggle with the innovation concept, you simultaneously show the complexity of the concept. This is not about you not being able to understand the innovation concept. It is about the fundamental problems of the concept that are reflected in the literature and that are relevant in a theory chapter. You just do it your own way.

Academic, Social, and Emotional Support

As shown in the dialogue, the feedback revolves around both identity and production. The construction of text is intimately connected to expressing a voice of experience based on gut feeling and on finding the right audience, on finding a place to be and to feel at home as a researcher. As illustrated, this peer group session included academic, social, and emotional support, as also reported by Lassig et al. (2013). Through supportive, but also tough, feedback, the peers provided both encouragement and challenges to the writer. They offered mutuality when referring to their own struggles and expertise when providing insights from their own fields of research, and they openly addressed issues of writer identity and the process of becoming a bona fide researcher. When the writer revealed her fears and doubts, her peers expressed their faith not only in her work but also in her ability to benefit from her creative personality and make a valuable and original contribution to her field of research.

Do I Have the Time . . . and the Courage?

Too Time-Consuming

Taking a break from one's own project to read others people's texts and meet with peers in writing groups may be unattractive because it is time-consuming. However, it should be borne in mind that all members of a peer group build expertise, mutuality, and identity, even though only one text is on the agenda at any given session. Building competencies as a peer reviewer is an important skill in academia, and a safe training environment reduces performance anxiety when the researcher eventually receives manuscripts for review from real journal editors. As a side effect, the reviewer role enables the student to decode what works well and to transfer these insights into his or her own writing. In our opinion, these benefits of peer group writing sessions should be supported by doctoral programs and by supervisors, even though the actual networking activities should remain the student's responsibility. The supervisor cannot, and should not, force the doctoral candidate to join a peer group. Nevertheless, what the supervisor can do is to emphasize a horizontal and distributed notion of apprenticeship learning.

Revealing Writings in Progress

Participation in peer groups can invite the doctoral student to reveal writings in progress and scrutinize how texts are developed during peer-review processes, shaped by and shaping researcher identity. One way of overcoming the problem of performance anxiety is to actually bring to the surface what we know but tend for forget in academia in our (often lonely) struggles with writing: namely, that most texts from both novice and experienced writers undergo substantial change during several rewriting processes. Most books and many research articles include acknowledgments, and while these might merely represent a formal courtesy, we are sure that most of them express genuine gratitude to people who have read the text in much less impressive versions—and who had the insight and power to give relevant and encouraging input to the rewriting process.

Nonproductive Peer Interaction

An important concern about peer groups, however, is that these are not supportive or productive per se. There are several potential negative outcomes of peer interaction, including over-intimacy, intrigues, and nonproductive power struggles. These kinds of peer group dynamics are obviously even more sensitive to report, especially from a first-person perspective. These aspects are important and need further attention as they may explain why some doctoral students are reluctant to participate or choose to withdraw from peer groups. The group dynamic in Charlotte's peer group suggests that a high degree of trust was essential to foster an environment in which both author and reviewers could talk openly and without any social positioning, due to the fact that the individuals were not part of the same research environment competing for the same positions. This kind of rapport usually takes some time to develop and may not always be accomplished. In this case, the important issue is to know when to break up the group. What we have aimed to demonstrate is the value of opening the door to the intimate room of peer learning and examining one way in which an academic text can be developed.

Life Itself Is a Master

As mentioned, there are several other resources of inspiration available to the doctoral student (as well as to the experienced researcher) in all phases of research processes. Many of them, however, are easily marginalized or ignored by doctoral students because they seem irrelevant or too intuitive, coincidental, or private to really count as "proper" research strategies. The student may be moving in a seemingly fruitful direction but still ask the professor if this is "the right way to do it."

The Memoir of a Nobel Prize Winner

The memoir *In Search of Memory* (Kandel, 2006) by Eric R. Kandel, who won the Nobel Prize in Medicine in 2000, may help. He tells the story of his scientific and private journey devoted to the study of memory, weaving together the personal and the scientific. His story displays the diverse influences and broad network of colleagues and friends involved in a genuine research life. In the introductory chapter, Kandel tells the story of his childhood in Vienna and his ninth birthday in 1938. He remembers the shiny blue remote-control model car he was given as a birthday present from his parents. He also remembers the two Nazi policemen entering the apartment two days later, ordering the Kandel family to pack a few things and leave their home immediately. After one frightening homeless year in Vienna, the Kandel family was able to leave for the United States. He can still recall details of things and sensations he experienced almost seventy years later:

> It is difficult to trace the complex interest and actions of one's adult life to specific experiences in childhood and youth. Yet I cannot help but link my later interest in mind—in how people behave, the unpredictability of motivation, and the persistence of memory—to my last year in Vienna. (Kandel, 2006, p. 5)

The direction of his motivation, however, was not straightforward. As a college student, he had an interest in contemporary Austrian and German history and planned to become an intellectual historian. Later, he developed a fascination for psychoanalysis and therefore decided to go to medical school. Less than a year later, the structure of the DNA was elucidated. It was then he began to think about exploring the mystery of learning and memory in biological terms. "How did the Viennese past leave its lasting traces in the nerve cells of my brain? How was the complex three-dimensional space of the apartment where I was steering my toy car woven into my brain's internal representation of the spatial world around me?" he asks. Additionally, several collaborators, students, and colleagues inspired him along the way, including his first mentor, the knowledgeable neurophysiologist Harry Grundfest, with whom he specifically sought to work: "All of this knowledge I had encountered in my basic science courses at New York University and in the assigned textbook readings, but none of it excited my curiosity or even meant much to me until Grundfest put it into context," Kandel (2006, p. 59) reflects. Thus, even a Nobel Prize winner's career pathway can be highly influenced by life itself: childhood experiences, historical circumstances in science and political life, and by influential encounters with significant others. What he did, and what we can learn from him, is to pay attention to all kinds of incidents, seek out potential masters, and acknowledge a wide range of inspirational forces in our lives.

Unscientific Method Chapters?

Dissertation method chapters, however, often report rational and chronological steps (Kamler & Thomson, 2008) while the actual process of getting to know something sparked by intuition, coincidence, or private incident is rarely mentioned. Likewise, epistemological struggle is regarded as something to be solved, with only the outcome worth reporting. It is our experience that students feel they have to create a narrative about what "really" happened because merely intuitive, coincidental, or serendipitous encounters and choices seem unscientific. However, as worded aptly in the history research textbook *Beyond the Archives*:

> Unless we pay serious attention to aspects of our lived experience that connect us with insight, intuition, and creativity, we might lose out on many leads that can enrich our understanding of past and present, virtual and historical experiences. And if new researchers censor this very real and useful aspect of the research process, they might not learn to trust or recognize their own hunches. That is not to say that serendipity is necessary for identifying a good research topic; in fact, coincidence, chance, or luck may not come into play at all. We consider genuine curiosity, a willingness to follow all possible leads, an openness to what one may encounter, and flexibility in revising research questions and the scope of a project to be key factors for conducting successful historical work. (Kirsch & Rohan, 2008, pp. 4–5)

Use Your Life Experience

This resonates well with Mills, who reminds the new doctoral student that the most admirable thinkers do not split their work from their lives: "They seem to take both too seriously to allow such dissociation, and they want to use each for the enrichment of the other" (Mills, 1952/1980, p. 1). What Mills teaches us is to learn to use our life experience in our intellectual work, to realize personal potentialities and acknowledge any opportunities that come in our way. But how can we do this? As mentioned in Chapter 3, Mills's answer is that we must set up a file or keep some kind of a journal for systematic reflection. In such a file one would include personal experience, professional activities, studies under way, and studies planned. Becker addresses similar issues using the metaphor of building a table out of different parts, not all of them his "own":

> If I need the idea for the table I'm building, I'll take it. It's still my table, even though some parts were prefabricated. I fact, I am so accustomed to working this way that I am always collecting such prefabricated parts for use in future arguments. Much of my reading is governed by a search for such useful modules . . . I also collect modules I have no present use for, when my intuition tells me I will eventually find the use. (Becker, 1986/2007, p. 146)

Knowledge Brokering

The idea of building your own reasoning and research projects based on things that are already there is given some, however scarce, attention in studies of innovation and creativity. "Knowledge brokering" (Hargadon, 2002; Hargadon & Sutton, 2000) is a term from management studies that is useful in the present context of doctoral learning. So this is both an explanation of a relevant term and a practical demonstration of a concept drawn from another domain. In management studies, the term *knowledge brokering* is used to explain how successful innovators systematically make use of old ideas as the raw material for new ones, thus stressing the role of interactions across organizations, professions, and domains as a core business strategy to enhance creativity and innovation. Knowledge brokering encourages people to "use their in-between vantage point to spot old ideas that can be used in new places, new ways, and new combinations" (Hargadon & Sutton, 2000, p. 58). A successful business innovation strategy is thus to capture ideas from a wide variety of sources, play with them, and imagine their use in other contexts (Tanggaard & Wegener, 2015). Hargadon (2002) notes that many definitions of creativity and innovation recognize the existence of old ideas, yet this point is often downplayed in efforts to identify and describe those events that produce revolutionary change. As a result, he states, dichotomic pairs using such terms as *revolutionary* vs. *evolutionary*, *radical* vs. *incremental*, and *discontinuous* vs. *continuous* are common. The problem is, however, that these descriptors often confuse the idea's impact with its origin. Accordingly, he argues that "revolutionary innovations often come from very evolutionary origins" (Hargadon, 2002, p. 51).

Pragmatic Ideals

Knowledge brokering is highly relevant for doctoral students and their supervisors (both in their role as master and as researcher). We have investigated the quest for originality in Chapter 3, and the ideas of knowledge brokering and distributed apprenticeship (extending beyond human-to-human interaction) add to this discussion. Wagner (2010) argues that budding scholars often have more grandiose ideals about doing *original* research and generating *new* knowledge than their faculty mentors will hold them to. However, "when it comes to the new knowledge ideal, students tend to aim for the stars and fear they'll never get there, whereas faculty members place one foot in front of the other and just move along" (Wagner, 2010, p. 31). His point is that pragmatic ideals of reducing ignorance and letting go of the quest for general truth claims provides doctoral students with a much more tangible and realistic ideal. Thus, the creative act as the production of new knowledge is the process of moving ideas from where they are known to where they are not. Sensitized to this gold mining mentality, we can consciously scan for peers and master (including ideas, artifacts, and experiences from our private lives) and transport these ideas from a foreign domain to our own research domain, thus finding novel application potential for them and reducing ignorance in our own (small) corner of the world.

Be a Master Yourself

The previous section was mainly occupied with "stealing." Another crucial part of a distributed notion of apprenticeship learning is *sharing*. The process of collecting ideas in solitude easily congeals and stagnates. Ideas need disturbance and add-ons. Mills puts it this way:

> What I also do myself is to share all of this with any relevant, potential future collaborators. Mails, text messages, a shared paper, everything that keeps ideas flowing, making them open to others' ideas energy will—eventually—make them crystallize into gold or garbage, or just on the way to become gold. (Mills, 1952/1980)

We call these "strategies to keep the ball rolling." When we get an idea in the middle of doing something to which the idea is not relevant or when we stumble upon a paper, a title, a quote, or anything that catches our attention as potentially worthwhile, we can make the ball roll with minimal effort. The ability to store is important, but equally important is the ability to put into circulation what we store to continually invest in the flow of knowledge creation. As we see it, these investments always yield dividends. The worst-case scenario is that you revisit "your" idea in a paper written by someone you have never spoken with (or worse—someone you did actually speak with), your name appearing nowhere. In our own experience, however, the annoyance about this apparent theft is abundantly overshadowed by the benefits of sharing. It is important, however, to gradually build networks wisely in order to test out and build relations of mutuality, veneration, and trust. That said, generosity is one of the most important researcher virtues, which not only elevates the creative processes but also prevents researcher gloom and deadlock. Times of isolation and cognitive stagnation are unavoidable, and generosity tends to be reciprocated. Sometimes, it is delayed, but that may be exactly the time when it is needed.

Good Advice for the PhD Student

- Take your time to seek out peers within and outside your field of research and home department. You might need different peer relations to support different aspects of your work and in different phases of your research project.
- Accept that it takes time to build trust and develop routines together. However, be aware that some peer relations will not work well, so allow yourself to break up with peers if necessary.
- Offer to give feedback on others peoples' texts and pay attention to what you can learn about writing from your own feedback practice.
- Be aware of the diverse range of inspirational sources in your social and institutional landscapes.
- Do not dismiss inspirational sources because you consider them to be inappropriate research strategies.
- Seek out strategies to keep the ball rolling by passing over ideas and investing in the flow of knowledge creation.

Good Advice for the Supervisor

- Emphasize a horizontal and distributed notion of apprenticeship learning by introducing potential peers to each other.
- Encourage your students to participate in a peer writing group.

- Suggest that your department offer a writing course each semester or initiate optional writing groups from time to time.
- Encourage the student to use life material as inspiration.
- Tell your students stories about your own creative strategies, happy incidents, and life experiences that turned out to influence your research in productive ways.

Conclusion

In this chapter, we have discussed the diverse range of learning resources beyond the formal supervisory relationship and advocated an apprentice-like state of mind. Writing from the outset and developing strategies for writing are essential throughout the doctoral journey and a means for both learning and production. Academic writing concerns knowledge production and dissemination, yet it is helpful to be aware that these processes are closely tied to scholarly identity formation. Through the lens of apprenticeship, writing is seen as a matter of gaining access to the trade in the field. One of the most important factors in successful completion is network, and in this chapter we have discussed peer learning and opened the door to the intimate room of a peer group workshop. Finally, we have looked at life experiences and the intuitive, coincidental, or private incidents that tend to be dismissed as relevant research material, and we have discussed ways in which ideas can be passed on and exchanged in the research community.

References

Aitchison, C., & Lee, A. (2006). Research writing: Problems and pedagogies. *Teaching in Higher Education, 11*(3), 265–278.

Aitchison, C., & Lee, A. (2010). Writing in, writing out: Doctoral writing as peer work. In M. Walker & P. Thomson (Eds.), *The Routledge doctoral supervisor's companion: Supporting effective research in education and the social sciences* (pp. 260–269). London: Routledge.

Badley, G. (2009). Academic writing as shaping and re-shaping. *Teaching in Higher Education, 14* (2), 209–219.

Baker, V. L., & Lattuca, L. R. (2010). Developmental networks and learning: Toward an interdisciplinary perspective on identity development during doctoral study. *Studies in Higher Education, 35*(7), 807–827.

Barley, S. R. (2006). When I write my masterpiece: Thoughts on what makes a paper interesting. *Academy of Management Journal, 49*(1), 16–20.

Becker, H. S. (1986/2007). *Writing for social scientists: How to start and finish your thesis, book, or article* (2nd ed.). London: University of Chicago Press.

Boud, D., & Lee, A. (2005). "Peer learning" as pedagogic discourse for research education. *Studies in Higher Education, 30*(5), 501–516.

Colyar, J. (2009). Becoming writing, becoming writers. *Qualitative Inquiry, 15*(2), 421–436.

Devenish, R., Dyera, S., Jeffersona, T., Lorda, L., van Leeuwena, S., & Fazakerleya, V. (2009). Peer to peer support: The disappearing work in the doctoral student experience. *Higher Education Research & Development, 28*(1), 59–70.

Fergie, G., Beeke, S., McKenna, C., & Creme, P. (2011). "It's a lonely walk": Supporting postgraduate researchers through writing. *International Journal of Teaching and Learning in Higher Education, 23*(2), 236–245.

Hargadon, A. B. (2002). Brokering knowledge: Linking learning and innovation. *Research in Organizational Behavior, 24*, 41–85.

Hargadon, A. B., & Sutton, R. I. (2000). Building an innovation factory. *Harvard Business Review, 78*(3), 157–166.

Hopwood, N. (2010). A sociocultural view of doctoral students' relationships and agency. *Studies in Continuing Education, 32*(2), 103–117.

Jazvac-Martek, M., Chen, S., & McAlpine, L. (2011). Tracking the doctoral student experience over time: Cultivating agency in diverse spaces. In L. McAlpine & C. Amundsen (Eds.), *Doctoral education: Research-based strategies for doctoral students, supervisors and administrators* (pp. 17–36). London: Springer.

Kamler, B. (2008). Rethinking doctoral publication practices: Writing from and beyond the thesis. *Studies in Higher Education, 33*(3), 283–294.

Kamler, B., & Thomson, P. (2008). The failure of dissertation advice books: Toward alternative pedagogies for doctoral writing. *Educational Researcher, 37*(8), 507–514.

Kandel, E. R. (2006). *In search of memory: The emergence of a new science of mind.* New York: W. W. Norton & Company.

Kirsch, G. E., & Rohan, L. (Eds.). (2008). *Beyond the archives: Research as a lived process.* Carbondale: Southern Illinois University Press.

Lassig, C. J., Dillon, L. H., & Diezmann, C. M. (2013). Student or scholar? Transforming identities through a research writing group. *Studies in Continuing Education, 35*(3), 299–314.

Lee, A., & Boud, D. (2003). Writing groups, change and academic identity: Research development as local practice. *Studies in Higher Education, 28*(2), 187–200.

Lockheart, J. (2010). How can we use writing as a tool for collaboration across disciplines at Ph.D. level?: Co-writing fictional versions of the truth about someone else. *Journal of Writing in Creative Practice, 3*(3), 299–315.

Maher, D., Seaton, L., McMullen, C., Fitzgerald, T., Otsuji, E., & Lee, A. (2008). "Becoming and being writers": The experiences of doctoral students in writing groups. *Studies in Continuing Education, 30*(3), 263–275.

Maher, M., Fallucca, A., & Mulhern Halasz, H. (2013). Write on! through to the Ph.D.: Using writing groups to facilitate doctoral degree progress. *Studies in Continuing Education, 35*(2), 193–208.

Malfroy, J. (2005). Doctoral supervision, workplace research and changing pedagogic practices. *Higher Education Research & Development, 24*(2), 165–178.

McAlpine, L., & Amundsen, C. (2007). Academic communities and developing identity: The doctoral student journey. In P. Richards (Ed.), *Global issues in higher education* (pp. 57–83). New York: Nova Publishing.

McAlpine, L., Paulson, J., Gonsalves, A., & Jazvac-Martek, M. (2012). "Untold" doctoral stories: Can we move beyond cultural narratives of neglect? *Higher Education Research & Development, 31*(4), 511–523.

Meier, N., & Wegener, C. (forthcoming). Writing with resonance: A dialogue on inspiration and voice in social science.

Mills, C. W. (1952/1980). On intellectual craftsmanship. *Society, 17*(2), 63–70.

Nordentoft, H. M., Thomsen, R., & Wichmann-Hansen, G. (2012). Collective academic supervision: A model for participation and learning in higher education. *Higher Education, 65*(5), 581–593.

Packer, M. J., & Goicoechea, J. (2000). Sociocultural and constructivist theories of learning: Ontology, not just epistemology. *Educational Psychologist, 35*(4), 227–241.

Pink, S. (2007). *Doing visual ethnography: Images, media and representation in research*. London: Sage.

Pink, S., Hubbard, P., O'Neill, M., & Radley, A. (2010). Walking across disciplines: From ethnography to arts practice. *Visual Studies, 25*(1), 1–7.

Richardson, L. (2003). Writing: A method of inquiry. In N. K. Denzin & Y. S. Lincoln (Eds.), *Collecting and interpreting qualitative materials* (2nd ed., pp. 499–541). Thousand Oaks, CA: Sage.

Tanggaard, L., & Wegener, C. (2015). Why novelty is overrated. *Journal of Education and Work,* ahead-of-print.

Wagner, J. (2010). Ignorance in educational research: How not knowing shapes new knowledge. In P. Thomson & M. Walker (Eds.), *The Routledge doctoral student's companion. Getting to grips with research in education and social sciences* (pp. 31–42). London: Routledge.

Walker, M., & Thomson, P. (Eds.). (2010). *The Routledge doctoral supervisor's companion: Supporting effective research in education and the social sciences*. London: Routledge.

Wegener, C., Meier, N., & Ingerslev, K. (2014). Borrowing brainpower—sharing insecurities. Lessons learned from a doctoral peer writing group. *Studies in Higher Education,* ahead-of-print, 1–14.

Wegener, C., & Tanggaard, L. (2013). Supervisor and student co-writing: An apprenticeship perspective. *Forum Qualitative Sozialforschung/Forum: Qualitative Social Research, 14*(3).

Weick, K. E. (1998). Introductory essay—improvisation as a mindset for organizational analysis. *Organization Science, 9*(5), 543–555.

Wright, T., & Cochrane, R. (2000). Factors influencing successful submission of PhD theses. *Studies in Higher Education, 25*(2), 181–195.

Chapter Six

Doing Supervision

Abstract

Purpose: The chapter takes the form of a narrative to illustrate how cowriting can become an integrated part of learning and supervising within doctoral studies.

Central message: The process of writing for publication is an effective way of gaining access and entering into the academic community. This is a process of both learning the craft of writing and developing researcher identity as long as the supervisor becomes involved in and builds on the students' ideas during a cowriting process.

Takeaways: The narrative makes visible ways in which the supervisor initially invites the student into the research community, provides access, and shows ways in which the student practices the craft through imitation and instruction, gradually becoming confident enough to make more decisions on her own.

Keywords: Cowriting, writing for publication, e-mails as data, "first-cut publisher," imitation, instruction, power dynamics, sharing and building power, "a pedagogy of doing."

Supervision as Process and Production

"Distributed" and "diverse," "peers" and "pathways" may obscure the significance of the supervisory relationship. There is a diverse range of learning resources, yet the collaboration between the doctoral student and their supervisor is fundamental. In this chapter we will look at the supervisory relationship as an activity involving mutual investment and joint agency. Supervision is not just something the supervisor *gives* and the doctoral student *receives* but something that recognizes student agency as being of major significance. Supervision involves both issues of production, a dissertation preferably of high quality and several other products (teaching material, conference presentations, and status reports), and issues of process (the student's socialization into a research community, lifelong learning, and identity formation) (Goode, 2010). Through the focus of this chapter—cowriting—we aim to address both. Through an e-mail exchange of our own, we aim to shed light on the process prior to and during a coauthored publication. It is highly contextual and person-specific. However, it can give rise to questions of how cowriting processes can be initiated and driven. What student attitudes and supervisor skills are required? How can cowriting become an integrated part of learning and supervising within doctoral study, and which potential disadvantages or hazards may be important along the way?

There is no "one size fits all," and the narrative in this chapter should be regarded as just one example of how one specific efficient and stimulating cowriting process evolved. It might inform a broader spectrum of doctoral students and supervisors to make their own informed choices about cowriting and their supervisory "doings."

The research on cowriting for production is sparse and evidence from processes that work appears to be ever sparser. There has been little empirical research on doctoral supervision practices and, despite a growing body of theoretical conceptualizations, supervision is still a privatized space or even a "black box" (Goode, 2010). This chapter is a revised version of a formerly published paper (Wegener & Tanggaard, 2013), that aims to open up this black box—which in this case is the mailbox—to one of our own supervisory *doings*.

Coauthorship as a Pedagogic Practice

Academic writing is complex, disciplined, and identity-related work, and it is not enough merely to offer a set of tips and tricks to increase output in narrow and short-term ways (Kamler, 2008; Kamler & Thomson, 2014). Issues around writing processes have been difficult to explore, and conversations about writing have inevitably favored product rather than process (Colyar, 2009). Doctoral writing can be regarded as a discursive social practice (Fairclough, 1992), as a form of discipline-specific social interaction embedded in institutions and social structures, yet with the researcher's engagement and investment in learning as a main driver. Through the lens of apprenticeship and with a perspective on learning as a matter of gaining access to the "trade" in the field, we consider cowriting as a core activity combining the aims for learning the craft of writing for publication with learning about one's topic of research. While writing, the researcher acquires new ideas and insights. Unfortunately, reflections, agreements, and advice during supervision are not necessarily remembered, transferred, or even understood by the student (which will be elaborated upon in Chapter 7). In contrast, a cowriting process continuously produces evidence of the student's experimenting with the material, struggling, and progressing. Learning the craft of writing manifests itself step by step in each version of the manuscript. Thus, the supervisor receives instant feedback about the student's learning, which is difficult to achieve from oral dialogue alone. Likewise, the student receives instant feedback from the supervisor's revisions and additions to the text and experiences the evolution of a tangible product of the learning process.

Literary apprenticeship is not new and has been formalized through writing classes and workshops at universities (Dawson, 2004, 48). While writing classes assist doctoral students with decoding the article format or with general requirements for dissertation chapters, they may not assist students in their struggle with the research material. From an apprenticeship perspective, however, pedagogics and practice "for real" are not independent of one another. Kamler (2008) argues that coauthorship with supervisors is a significant pedagogic practice that can enhance the robustness and know-how of emerging scholars as well as their publication output. There is a need, however, to rethink coauthorship more explicitly as a pedagogic practice, particularly in the humanities and social sciences.

E-Mails as Real-Time Data

Wolcott (1990) discusses the usefulness and importance of "writing early." He argues that writing about our work provides a baseline, an articulation of where we have been as researchers. This emphasizes the importance of field notes about assumptions and impressions during the process of analysis. The e-mails in the present chapter are not created as early writings or conscious field notes about process. However, unintended as they may be, they constitute a comprehensive record of learning and collaboration, because each exchange of a new manuscript version is followed by a commentary e-mail.

McMorland et al. (2003) note that collective reflection on the practice of doctoral supervision remains underdeveloped amongst the community of academic supervisors and students, and few studies inquire into practice "from the inside." Our empirical material does not express conscious reflection or focused baseline construction. However, we apply them here as retrospective reflections and for this purpose, they serve as glimpses into the main features of supervision, learning, and production through cowriting.

E-mails as data imbedded in communities is comprehensively discussed by, for example, Orlikowski and Yates, who analyzed almost 2,000 e-mail messages revealing certain aspects of a community's organizing process (Orlikowski & Yates, 1994, p. 570). Based on the notion of communities of practice (Brown & Duguid, 1991; Lave & Wenger, 1991), Orlikowski and Yates (1994) claim that e-mails are communicative actions situated in a social practice that shapes and is shaped by individuals. E-mails have also been used as data, with the aim of analyzing unity and diversity in a cross-university collaboration project (Akkerman, Admiraal, & Simons, 2012). They also represent what is currently a very typical medium for research communication, serving as a supplement or alternative to face-to-face meetings, and in this regard, this particular e-mail communication reveals a supervisory process as it occurred in this increasingly common meeting of virtual reality and research.

The Coauthor Study

The empirical data for this study comprises 55 e-mails, which represent the complete communication related to a published book chapter and an article, as we did not discuss these coauthored works at our physical meetings. The 23 e-mails (translated from Danish) presented in the following analysis have been selected and shortened with the aim of conveying the main features of apprenticeship during a process of combined doctoral supervision and cowriting.

The following e-mail dialogues involve Lene (the supervisor), Charlotte (the student), and David Boud (the editor of the journal). We present the e-mails in chronological order to highlight the dynamics and progress of the interaction: the critical parts in the student's writing process, her views about the work, how she asks more or less directly for help, and how the supervisor handles her response—sometimes with contributions to the text and sometimes by giving instructions to encourage the student to proceed on her own. As such, the analysis takes the form of a narrative in order to illustrate an apprentice–master interaction. This process makes visible the initial invitation to the research community; the provison of access; and the apprentice's learning the craft through imitation and instruction, gradually becoming confident enough to make more decisions on her own. The narrative also indicates that access is never fully accomplished, as there is always a new or wider community in which to become involved and that the quest for credibility goes on.

Inviting in—Unconditionally Accepting

25 August 2011 16:08 Lene Tanggaard wrote:

Dear Charlotte

Today I was asked to contribute to a book on Innovation Psychology. There is a short time available, and the final manuscript must be ready in December. However, it struck me that maybe we could write the manuscript together?

Alternatively, I can write it myself, but it would be great with an empirical article based on your interviews.

Please consider it but I understand if you turn it down, of course.

Regards,
Lene

25 August 2011 16:24 Charlotte Wegener wrote:

Hi Lene

I don't need to think about it. Of course I would like to do it. How do we start?

Charlotte

25 August 2011 16:35 Lene Tanggaard wrote:

Hi Charlotte

Super! I can do a big chunk of the theory—set the psychological framework. So you do a draft and I take over? And then we can send it back and forth by email and talk it over.

Best regards,
Lene

This e-mail communication pinpoints the initial step in the apprentice-learning process of how to craft an academic paper. However, there is no instruction given from the supervisor about how to initiate this work, no information provided about editorial requirements or text format. Being a member of a research community, the supervisor is capable of facilitating a kind of "open sesame" to provide access to her community with just one e-mail query to the student. She knows the student's empirical material and initial analysis and emphasizes the student's contribution (empirical material), making clear its potential value. She also specifies her own contribution (the theoretical framework). The student is recognized for her work so far and responds to this with unconditional acceptance and a fundamental question: how to begin? The supervisor frames the collaborative process: "We can send it back and forth by email" and hands over the initiative to the student: "You do a draft."

Idea Testing and Getting the Student to Work

The student completes a draft, suggesting that her empirical material reveals two distinct perceptions of innovation: levers that are understood as methods, techniques, and management detached from the daily work practices; and craft, understood as professional skills bounded in actual work situations where ideas emerge and problems must be solved:

28 August 2011 14:13 Charlotte Wegener wrote:

Hi Lene,

Here are some initial ideas. It feels good to get started so here is a raw sketch. It will be easier for me to continue when I see your suggestion for a theoretical framework.

What about the target group? What role should the empirical material play? I have blocked my calendar all Friday for writing.

Regards,
Charlotte

28 August 2011 15:18 Lene Tanggaard wrote:

Hi Charlotte,

Impressive—I love your analytical distinction between innovation as 'craft' and as 'levers'. Both conceptions of innovation are valid, but we could emphasise the importance of linking craft and levers if innovation is to change practice for real. I can frame the chapter, outline the dominant theories of creativity and set the scene for our approach. However, I don't have time the next couple of days.

The empirical material should play the leading role—that indicates that we are really conducting research.

If you have the time, you can describe the method before I take over.

Regards,
Lene

This dialogue takes place only three days later. And for a reason: The student is quick to present her main idea to prevent performance anxiety, and to avoid potential critique, she mentions that this piece of writing is just a rough sketch. She also asks for feedback to test the idea about different understandings of innovation as craft and levers, and she also asks for the supervisor's theoretical input and seeks advice about the audience. Finally, she demonstrates her commitment by telling the supervisor that she is devoting substantial time to the research. The supervisor is very supportive, praises the work so far, and suggests a theme—a main hypothesis to guide the student's work. She also leaves additional work to be done by the student before she takes over. Gentle pressure and a few guidelines are provided.

Theoretical Framing

The student writes a draft of the method chapter as advised, and shortly after, the supervisor does what she promised and returns a new version with the theoretical framing:

1 September 2011 10:25 Lene Tanggaard wrote:

Dear Charlotte

I have given the chapter a thorough theoretical going-over. Actually, it was fun to clarify that we are continuing the latest trend within the psychological creativity and innovation research, and also taking it a step further through qualitative empirical study.

You are welcome to complement and comment. I have inserted some references. It is important that we specify the main themes in the concluding discussion. Please think along those lines and send back the chapter when you have worked with it.

Kind regards,
Lene

The supervisor has now made a major contribution to the manuscript where she clarifies their shared theoretical foundation and contribution to the research field. She invites the student to add more and takes stock of the remaining tasks to be completed. She restates central issues and advises the student to keep these in mind when proceeding.

2 September 2011 19:02, Charlotte Wegener wrote:

Hi Lene

Here is what I have achieved so far. I have rearranged some sections without tracking changes, but all new text is tracked. I have not worked on the discussion yet, but I have tried to emphasise the themes in the Introduction. When we have decided more precisely on the themes, I will go through the analysis again.

Have a nice weekend - Charlotte

4 September 2011 22.25 Lene Tanggaard wrote:

Hi Charlotte

You have made some good additions! When you rewrite the empirical analysis, try to make use of our introductory theory. Like: "This resembles N's definition of . . ." and "Here are clear parallels to . . ." This allows for a dynamic reading process and our introductory reflections will explicitly guide the reader through the empirical data. Theory and data will both challenge and verify each other. You might also rephrase some quotes and include them in the body of the text.

Best regards
Lene

The student feels uncertain about how to proceed in making theory and empirical data interact. She rearranges some sections and adds text, but she hesitates to finally decide on the analytical themes and arguments. She implicitly asks the supervisor to be involved in the decision making as she writes "when we have decided more precisely on the themes . . ." The supervisor, however, does not respond to this call but instructs the student by suggesting specific wordings and phrasings that might help her to proceed on her own.

Focused Asking for Advice and Making Structural Adjustments

9 September 2011 13:32 Charlotte Wegener wrote:

Hi Lene,

Now the manuscript needs a good think.

I will comment on the model on the last page if you think it makes sense. I am not happy with the analytical categories/headings, but I will take a look at them in the next round.

Additionally, I need relevant literature about couplings and decouplings. It is not quite the same as "points of coupling" is it?

The mental side (innovation as thinking) is empirically significant. What part of the creativity literature deals with this?

I have time to work during the weekend.

Kind regards,
Charlotte

10 September 2011 17:23 Lene Tanggaard wrote:

Dear Charlotte

I have written a clear introduction—it was missing. I have made some minor adjustments to the theoretical part. I have referred to Bilton to highlight the celebration of the new within the innovation discourse.

It really works now. The interview quotes are funny (or tragi-comic). It is fine to use my concept "decoupling"—I suggest that you refer to it briefly where you mention Engeström.

In my opinion, the strength of the empirical material is that is shows that the innovation concept tends to be decoupled from professional practice and its values. It is both an advantage and a disadvantage—mostly the latter.

In my opinion, the informants' focus on thinking reveals the prevalence of the classic psychological model of creativity as divergent thinking (I have added a few sentences on that). Additionally, we could emphasise the need to develop creativity models, which does not just deal with thinking, but includes questions on how to make things happen, how to integrate innovation into professional contexts, how to make creativity meaningful in relation to values, ethics and professionalism. The decoupling of the creativity concept from these additional concepts is the main problem.

Your idea to introduce the empirical sections with a diagram is good. The model in the final section works well—we could use it earlier to prevent an abrupt closure. It might be better conclude with the abovementioned decoupling problem.

I can look through the text once more, but we are almost there.

Regards,
Lene

This dialogue reveals the student's impatience and dissatisfaction. She has worked as instructed, made a model displaying the analytical themes, and made decisions about headlines to organize the themes. She effectively presents one of the main themes in the empirical material (the understanding of innovation as a mental process), and she is able to specify her needs (help with definitions and theory to qualify this finding). She knows what is missing, but she cannot complete the analysis herself at the moment, or perhaps she is unnecessarily self-critical. It appears, in fact, that the supervisor feels that only small adjustments are needed, as shown in the following correspondence. However, the manuscript needs "oxygen"—and so does the student. The supervisor knows that the paper is almost ready for submission and makes some small adjustments. Additionally, she moves to another level of abstraction through commenting on their theoretical contribution to the research field. She thus indicates that creative investigation and introspective learning are no longer enough. Now, it is time to consider the form of presentation, the strengthening of arguments, and their positioning in a wider community of practice:

Fine-Tuning and Some Deletions

14 September 2011 22:28 Lene Tanggaard wrote:

Dear Charlotte,

I have made some small changes and deleted a section prior to the method chapter. Is that okay? I think it was a bit too chatty . . . but if you really want to, we can keep it.

Regards,
Lene

15 September 2011 10:21 Charlotte Wegener wrote:

Hi again

The deletion is fine. I have done a language check, and if you find it ready for submission, we submit.

See you tomorrow—thank you for pushing me.

Regards,
Charlotte

Until now, the supervisor has refrained from deleting any of the student's writing. Instead, she has guided the wording by adding to the manuscript or by identifying the main theoretical themes in the e-mails. This gentle support has allowed the student to develop her personal "stamp," an angle on the research problem (Kamler & Thomson, 2006) and a "writer stance" (Hyland, 2002), and from the supervisor perspective, it was indeed intended to be just that. There were probably other "chatty" sections, but the student removed some of them along the way, while developing her ideas through writing and rewriting and while exercising the craft of academic writing. The rest is left to the reviewers. The student is feeling rather self-confident for the time being and accepts the deletion with ease, and clearly appreciates the supervisor's initial "push." This wording reveals the delicate balance between providing access to the research community and expecting the student to contribute. Access and guidance are not provided once and for all but must come in measured, situational doses—occasionally specific and firm—while space and trust are required at other times.

Sharing Completion

The manuscript has now been submitted and the next e-mail addresses the reviews:

2 October 2011 10:07 Lene Tanggaard wrote

Dear Charlotte

The feedback is quite good. Congratulations to you (and me)—I know from John [a colleague who also submitted a paper] that some reviewer comments were very tough, so we are lucky . . .

Do you want to look through it to ensure a nuanced discussion and conclusion? These are minor requests. I will take a look at it afterwards.

By the way, let's do our own revision and develop the paper further. I think we could develop our overall conception of innovation and learning even further and write about it for a more international audience. We will discuss that later.

Kind regards,
Lene

2 October 2011 17:13 Charlotte Wegener wrote:

Hi Lene

Here is an attempt to meet the editors' requests. We still need to include the role of psychology and the fact that we are trying to complement the management research.

Something has been replaced; something is new.

Best regards,
Charlotte

After a second revision, the book chapter is accepted for publication, and e-mails concerning other tasks pile up in the mailboxes until

14 November 2011 09:54 Lene Tanggaard wrote:

Dear Charlotte

At some point, we should develop our paper further and publish it more internationally. The journal *Studies in Continuing Education* is an obvious choice. Moreover, it is ranked second on the bibliometric research indicator, so you will be well positioned if we succeed.

Regards,
Lene

In the first e-mail, the supervisor congratulates the student and leaves the revision to her, reassuring her that it entails minor requests and she promises to look through it afterwards. The student gains experience about responding to reviews and the supervisor frees up time for other tasks. The book chapter is completed, but there is no time for complacency while the work is still fresh and current.

Extending the Radius of the Research Community

The supervisor assesses the material as worthy of further publication and now offers the student access to the international research community. However, this is unmanageable and vague to the student, and she does not respond to the initial request, so a "bait" from academia is mentioned, namely the bibliometric research indicator. As the final e-mail conversation in this paper reveals, the two of them indeed managed to continue the further cooperative development of the paper:

1 December 2011 08:50 Charlotte Wegener wrote:

Hi Lene,

I managed to upload the manuscript. It took some time but practice makes perfect, I guess. ☺

Regards,
Charlotte

12 May 2012 10:57

To: Charlotte Wegener

Subject: Studies in Continuing Education—Decision on Manuscript ID CSCE-2011-0060

Dear Ms. Wegener:

We have now received responses from the referees to your paper 'Educational Innovation: A Craft or a Lever?' submitted to *Studies in Continuing Education*. My apologies for the delay, we needed to approach many referees before finding some suitable ones.

They recommend that your paper be published subject to revision. The reviewer comments are included at the bottom of this email.

Sincerely,
David Boud

16 May 2012 15:23 Lene Tanggaard wrote:

Dear Charlotte

The review is quite positive and we are almost there. It is a good idea to read the suggested articles. Both reviewers ask for a more focused literature review regarding innovation/elder care/public sector. The first reviewer even did some of our work for us by referring to specific articles. I'll take care of the concepts "craft" and "levers. They also suggest that we have a new title, which is a good idea.

Let's keep in touch . . . I won't start writing until I get your "go ahead," but I will read and reflect.

Regards,
Lene

19 May 2012 15:33 Charlotte Wegener wrote:

Hi Lene

This is my preliminary revision. The paper needs to be reorganised to give the model a more prominent position, but I need to get a better grip on the contents first. However, you may find a brutal cut and paste simple and know what to do? If so, please do it.

We need to cut about 2,500 words (required maximum length is 8,000 words).

The title gets weirder the more I try, so I'll leave it for a while.

Regards,
Charlotte

21 May 2012 09:25 Lene Tanggaard wrote:

Dear Charlotte

You have made some great changes. I have added quite a lot. I have tried to clarify our aim and stress that human creativity is a prerequisite for successful innovation. By doing so, craft and creativity are linked (which is a little funny, per se). Maybe even more clarification is needed, but we are almost there. The learning dimension is clarified too.

I have deleted the introductory quotation and therefore deleted the reference to it in the discussion. I have deleted the section about Grounded Theory; I think the paper works well without it. New title—what do you think?

All changes are with track changing mode and still changeable, of course.

Kind regards,
Lene

Although reduced in some sections, the manuscript is now too extensive, and for the first time the student makes deletions in text written by the supervisor. From the classroom, attending an optional course about research strategies for doctoral students, she writes:

21 May 2012 15:40 Charlotte Wegener wrote:

Dear Lene

I have removed around 1,300 words. If you cut another 1,000, we are within the limit. I have added information about the actors and the interview guide. I am listening to a lecture about how to write popular science articles . . .

Regards,
Charlotte

The student does not comment on her selection criteria, instead focusing on the shared efforts at streamlining the manuscript. Additionally, she makes a discreet joke about the irrelevance of a lecture, which aims at improving her writing skills, while she simultaneously improves her writing skills for "real."

A Pedagogy of Doing

We will now turn to potentially generalizable knowledge that can be extracted from this specific cowriting process. Critical perspectives on cowriting will be considered along with some methodological reservations. Finally, we shall list key advantages and pitfalls of student–supervisor cowriting and suggest how doctoral supervision within an apprenticeship perspective can be carried out through cowriting.

To sum up, what is perhaps most evident from our own process is the relatively brief and implicit style of the supervisor. Even if the e-mail conversation gives the impression of continuous and elaborate conversation, the paper is actually written on the basis of a relatively small set of virtual interactions. It is written through the process of working together, based on an implicit and mutual understanding of writing and getting things done. What is required to write and get published is not always elicited verbally, detached from the actual everyday process of writing and trying to publish. It lies in the activity itself and is sometimes seen more clearly and precisely by both supervisor and student when they engage in the activity together. Additionally, there is undoubtedly an interest from both parties in getting the work done, as both are dependent on publishing their work. In this light, cowriting must be seen as a mutual investment and, accordingly, as yielding mutually benefits. Students serve as data-providers and publishing motors, and students who really learn the craft contribute to more publications, both while learning and over the longer term. This shared understanding creates a no-nonsense alignment and common purpose, which allows the supervisor to be quite explicit about production expectations and at the same time allows the student a fair amount of the supervisor's time and attention. The student gets the opportunity to decode academic writing conventions while reading the supervisory contribution, and at the same time, she is on her own to practice and thus has the opportunity to become a critical, creative researcher. She does not have to worry that she might "put her foot in it," as she can leave the initial assessment of her ideas and writing style to the supervisor. Gradually, she gains increased knowledge on how to operate in terms of publishing discourses.

The "First-Cut Publisher"

Her own judgments are thus not critical in this phase, because the supervisor acts as a gatekeeper:

> The term *first-cut publisher* evokes an understanding of the supervisor as a critical mediator and representative of the broader scholarly community, embodying its conventions, reading the text to help it stand up in the international arena. Again, it is the supervisor who keeps the student in the game (Kamler, 2008, 290).

Accordingly, studies have shown that coauthorship with supervisors is significant in developing a profile for student writing in both education and science research communities. It is coauthorship that produces internationally refereed publications—without it, they would not exist (Kamler, 2008, p. 292). Coauthorship helps students progressing through the struggles and anxieties of publishing and shares the experience of acceptance or rejection. This fosters the student's ability to cope and be robust within the social practice of academic work. In our own coauthorship narrative, it is evident that the supervisor serves as an accomplice during the review processes, and despite the fact that reviewers' comments might sound harsh, the student is not alone in receiving them, decoding them, and returning to the manuscript and revising in order to meet the requirements. As mentioned, the present analysis is based on only 55 e-mails from a single coauthorship process and thus, represents evidence from only one single supervisor–student relationship. Each supervisor-student relationship is unique and may also change over time and reveal diverse aspects, depending on the actual shared task. As such, several reservations in terms of generalization must be made.

Advantages and Pitfalls

There are both advantages and potential pitfalls integral to cowriting processes. What worked well in this case might be dysfunctional in others. For example, the rather brief and implicit supervisory style that encouraged the student in our case may block other students, and thus more instruction or explicit guidance may be what it takes. Although a dominant practice within the sciences, this kind of guidance has been perceived negatively, particularly in the field of education, for ethical reasons regarding questions of ownership, autonomy, and self-exploration (Kamler, 2008, p. 285). A general criticism of apprenticeship is that it entails the risk of reproduction and intellectual conformity (Walker et al., 2008, p. 90). These reservations should, of course, be taken into consideration during a cowriting process, as well as in all other activities that fall within doctoral supervision. Collaboration always involves power dynamics, and when the collaborators have uneven access to power it may be even more important to keep the question of power and ethics in mind and for the supervisor to act accordingly. The student might not feel safe enough or be too focused on doing well in academia to express feelings of being overruled. Thus, we believe that the supervisor has the power and even an obligation to continually become involved in and build on the students' ideas during a cowriting process. Additionally, is seems important (as the supervisor does in one of the e-mails) to invite the student explicitly to revise the supervisor's writing. Cowriting should not be the merging of two authors' texts; rather, it should end up being one product with two personal "stamps," and a shared angle on the research problem, as mentioned by Kamler and Thomson (2006).

Sharing and Building of Power

From this perspective, what is often neglected in reservations towards coauthorship seems to be the sharing and building of power inherent to a cowriting process. From an apprenticeship perspective, the power of production and the sharing of a goal (and not goals invented by the supervisor to construct artificial milestones for the student) somewhat evens out the power balance. Doctoral writers need to learn how to adopt an authoritative stance in a field of "expert others," and to assert their contributions to that field before they feel authoritative themselves (Kamler, 2008, p. 286). Coauthoring supports this process by lending power to the student—power that empowers the student subsequently, or simultaneously, to work toward publishing alone and with peers.

The apprenticeship learning perspective sheds light on how the process of getting published is a way of gaining access and entering into the academic community. This is a process of both learning the craft and developing researcher identity. From this point onwards, cowriting is likely to yield a steep learning curve for the student, enhance the effectiveness of the time spent on supervision, and produce a research article of high quality. It would be both interesting and instructive for future doctoral supervisors, students, and doctoral program providers to produce and have access to more research that delves into the dynamics of cowriting. Data for such research could take the form of students and supervisors keeping diaries, interview studies, or retrospectively reviewing published coauthored papers, in order to identify and analyze patterns within student–supervisor interaction.

Good Advice for the PhD Student

- Involve yourself in all parts of the job, including those parts that are unpleasant.
- Accept that writing takes time and involves hard work.
- Don't aim at over-performing or impressing; just send a version before you are satisfied—or at least before you feel like giving up.
- Tell your supervisor what you need in order to keep your spirits up.
- If you don't know what you need, tell your supervisor that you don't know.
- "Getting your hands dirty" from the start avoids performance anxiety and creates concrete (text) material with which to work. Writing is rewriting, and cowriting involves sharing both ideas and concerns.

Good Advice for the Supervisor

- Encourage rapid exchanges of written material.
- Redirect or advise the student with minimal effort and small hints, which maintains morale and the speed of writing.
- Tell the student what works well.
- Wait on deletions (except pure mistakes and misconceptions).
- Help in deciphering reviewer comments.
- Invite the student to cowrite a "cowriting diary" for future research on student and supervisor cowriting!

Conclusion

Throughout the chapters of this book, our advice has been that doctoral processes include interaction with a diverse range of people and with as many collaborators as possible or as required by the student. As mentioned, in the case of supervision, apprenticeship teaching is often practiced as private, one-to-one interactions between the supervisor and the student (Walker et al., 2008). Golde and Walker (2006) argue that doctoral education programs should be structured to prepare students as "stewards of the discipline"—scholars who imaginatively generate new knowledge and critically conserve valuable ideas—but also transform such new understandings through writing, teaching, application, and of course, publication. Students cannot do all of this on their own or with the supervisor as their only source of inspiration. Doctoral programs and doctoral courses that encourage cowriting and, in general, collaboration with different mentors and peers are surely to be favored. There is a diverse range of learning resources, yet the collaboration between the doctoral students and their supervisors is fundamental. In this chapter we have looked at the supervisory relationship as an activity involving mutual investment and joint agency. As illustrated, doctoral supervision within an apprenticeship perspective can be carried out through cowriting as an effective strategy for both learning the craft of writing and developing researcher identity. Cowriting is a supervisory activity that recognizes student agency and involves both issues of production and issues of process that are relevant for both parties.

References

Akkerman, S. F., Admiraal, W., & Simons R. J. (2012). Unity and diversity in a collaborative research project. *Culture & Psychology, 18*(2), 227–252.

Brown, J. S., & Duguid, P. (1991). Organizational learning and communities-of-practice: Toward a unified view of working, learning, and innovation. *Organization Science, 2*(1), 40–57.

Colyar, J. (2009). Becoming writing, becoming writers. *Qualitative Inquiry, 15*(2), 421–436.

Dawson, P. (2004). *Creative writing and the new humanities.* London: Routledge.

Fairclough, N. (1992). *Discourse and social change.* Cambridge: Polity Press.

Golde, C. M., & Walker, G. E. (2006). *Envisioning the future of doctoral education: Preparing stewards of the discipline.* San Francisco, CA: Carnegie Essays on the Doctorate, Jossey-Bass–Carnegie Foundation for the Advancement of Teaching.

Goode, J. (2010). Student agency in "doing supervision." In M. Walker & T. Pat (Eds.), *The Routledge doctoral supervisor's companion: Supporting effective research in education and the social sciences* (pp. 38–50). London: Routledge.

Hyland, K. (2002). Authority and invisibility: Authorial identity in academic writing. *Journal of Pragmatics, 34*(8), 1091–1112.

Kamler, B. (2008). Rethinking doctoral publication practices: Writing from and beyond the thesis. *Studies in Higher Education, 33*(3), 283–294.

Kamler, B., & Thomson, P. (2006). *Helping doctoral students write: Pedagogies for supervision.* London: Routledge.

Kamler, B., & Thomson, P. (2014). *Helping doctoral students write: Pedagogies for supervision.* Oxon: Routledge.

Lave, J., & Wenger, E. (1991). *Situated learning: Legitimate peripheral participation.* Cambridge: Cambridge University Press.

McMorland, J., Carroll, B., Copas, S., et al. (2003). Enhancing the practice of PhD supervisory relationships through first- and second-person action research/peer partnership inquiry. *Forum Qualitative Sozialforschung/Forum: Qualitative Social Research*, 4.

Orlikowski, W. J., & Yates, J. (1994). Genre repertoire: The structuring of communicative practices in organizations. *Administrative Science Quarterly, 39*(4), 541–574.

Walker, G. E., Golde, C. M., Jones, L., et al. (2008). *The formation of scholars: Rethinking doctoral education for the twenty-first century.* San Francisco, CA: Jossey-Bass.

Wegener, C., & Tanggaard, L. (2013). Supervisor and Student Co-Writing: An Apprenticeship Perspective. *Forum Qualitative Sozialforschung/Forum: Qualitative Social Research 14* (3).

Wolcott, H. F. (1990). On seeking—and rejecting—validity in qualitative research. In E. W. Eisner & A. Peshkin (Eds.), *Qualitative inquiry in education: The continuing debate* (pp. 121–152). New York: Teachers College Press.

Chapter Seven

Feedback—
Part of Making It Work

Abstract

Purpose: The purpose of the present chapter is to show and discuss different opportunities for dialogue and ways to obtain other people's reactions to our work.

Central message: Feedback involves exposure to criticism. Nevertheless, feedback is a crucial source for moving forward and should not be postponed until we feel that our thoughts and our texts are finished.

Takeaways: Getting feedback from a broader audience and learning to give appreciative feedback ourselves are part of research life and keys to deep involvement in the research community. Asking for feedback involves risk; however, it can also free the writer from aiming at a "perfect" text from the outset.

Keywords: Feedback, meta-analysis, a broader view, formative assessment, boundary crossing, horizontal learning, conflicting voices, pressure to publish, rewriting, dialogue, defensive writing, risking, disclosure of chaos.

A Range of Options

We have dealt with feedback of different kinds as part of peer learning processes in Chapter 5 and within cowriting strategies in Chapter 6. In this chapter, we devote our attention exclusively to feedback and the craft of asking for, benefitting from, and giving feedback. Supervisory feedback is essential for the student's progress and for the completion of a dissertation. Besides this, there is a range of options for dialogue and means of obtaining others' reactions to your work. Feedback can be the product of collaboration and discussions with a colleague, or of lecturing or presenting a paper at a conference. In a recent review of workplace learning studies, Noe, Clark, and Klein (2014) say that access to feedback enhances self-awareness, increases the individual's confidence regarding performance and success, and helps alleviate the stress associated with challenging work experiences.

How, where, and to what end should doctoral students seek out the feedback they need at specific times? How should they deal with serious criticism and make the feedback a source for moving forward? In *Sjælens Amerika*, the Norwegian author Karl Ove Knausgaard (2013) devoted an entire chapter to the issue of the exchange of feedback between peers and editors in the process of writing. He explains how, over time, the author and the editor almost become one voice. The editor is the shadow, the often invisible guide and sometimes the actual ghost-writer: "The job of editor is performed in a type of shadow cast by the name of the author" (Knausgaard, 2013, p. 377). In doctoral training, the supervisor can be closely involved, but while professional editors are often experienced in helping a text come across more clearly, a doctoral supervisor is given the role as supervisor on the background of her own expertise in the topic of research. While she may herself be a good writer, it does not follow that she will also be an excellent "midwife" for the student's texts and research contributions. In the following, various examples of access to feedback and the processes of writing with and learning from feedback will be discussed.

A Good Writer Is Not Necessarily a Good Writing Teacher

Through observations and recordings of supervisory sessions complemented by interviews, Paré (2010) found that supervisor feedback is often ambiguous, enigmatic, and difficult to understand. He notes that supervisors' ability to write well does not necessarily qualify them to impart the art of good writing. As language is often learned as a by-product of participation in particular activities—academic language being no exception—good academic writers may not be able to explain the reason for their advice. They may be unable or unaware of the need to explain why "they suggest or demand that something be phrased in a certain way, expect a particular tone or style, insist that a specific reference be inserted, or favour a certain way of organizing and presenting data over another" (Paré, 2010, p. 109). Paré found that supervisors in his study spoke with authority about what should be done to make students' writing move forward. The advice was potentially useful but often unelaborated and thus difficult for the students to understand and translate into a better product. What students need to understand—and what supervisors could be better at explaining—is that supervisory feedback is part of an enculturation process. Through writing and feedback, the student learns more about the community they are entering. Since the supervisor is a member of that community, he or she is one of the main resources on which students can draw when becoming scholars. Thus, if a supervisor does not articulate the feedback clearly with reference to the rules and rhetoric of the discipline, the student can ask for explanations. According to Paré (2010), this will strengthen the students' ability to engage in meta-analysis about both the relevance and value of their work and about the culture within which such judgments are made.

Feedback From an Apprenticeship Perspective

With respect to apprenticeship in doctoral training, the issue of giving and receiving feedback can be approached from a decentralized perspective. When writing about assessment in an apprenticeship learning perspective, Lave and Wenger (1991) underline that sources of feedback are distributed in the communities of practice in which the apprentice participates. Opportunities for feedback are to be found not only in the relation between apprentice and master but also through participation in the broader community, through the tasks undertaken and, for example, amongst peers and students. As underlined by Paré (2010) in the above, the student must learn about the culture of research in order to gain a broader view from the variety of feedback received. Lave and Wenger assert that access "to sources for understanding happens through growing involvement" (Lave & Wenger, 1991, p. 37). As they put it, "A learning curriculum unfolds its opportunities for engagement in practice. It is not specified as a set of dictates for proper practice" (Lave & Wenger, 1991, p. 93). In this sense, feedback in doctoral training from an apprenticeship perspective is to be understood as opportunities for guidance that arise through growing involvement. We received one very precise description of how this happens from one of our colleagues, Klaus Nielsen, when we asked him to name some defining moments in his doctoral training.

Klaus' Story About His Supervisor

In the following, I will briefly outline some of the things I learned from my supervisor, when I was PhD student. I have tried to use some of the things I learned from my supervisor since I was employed at the university and had to supervise PhD students of my own. The story I present below concerns an incident in which I found I learned a lot by working together with my supervisor. The point I want to make is that it is important to question some of the standard ways we work as supervisors.

In 1994, the PhD programme had just been inaugurated in Denmark and I had been accepted as a PhD student. My supervisor was a respected professor whom I had known for some years. He had already advised me on my Master's thesis and now became my PhD supervisor. I was his first PhD student, and, in many respects, when I began as a doctoral student, we resumed the same kind of relationship we had before when I was working on my Master's thesis. I will give a short account of how the supervision relationship worked. I made a plan for my dissertation clarifying what kind of theoretical and empirical work I needed to do to finish my dissertation on time. Whenever I needed supervision, I would contact my supervisor. A couple of days before we met, I would send him the textual material I wanted him to read and comment on. We would meet and he would make some comments about the material I had sent him. In most cases, he would have a number of critical comments about possible improvements and might add a few (educational) positive comments about the strengths and importance of the material I was working on. This would be the standard interaction, which most of our supervision meetings were constructed around; to be honest, I do not remember much about these meetings. To this day, I can hardly remember any of the comments he made about my papers, but I am sure I integrated most of them in my work.

Quite incidentally, something occurred that changed our relationship, and this had a significant impact on me. My supervisor and I were both working in the same field—learning in practice. By coincidence, I heard that a colleague we both knew was about to submit a paper to a journal. I happened to be preparing a paper on more or less the same topic and was planning to send my paper to the same journal. My supervisor had written about the same topic earlier, so I jokingly suggested to him that we could make a special issue on this topic in the journal, because we had at least two contributions and potentially three, if my supervisor would re-write the piece he had published earlier. My supervisor immediately refused the idea because, as he said, he "was drowning in work." I thought that was the end of that story—however, the next day my supervisor arrived at my office and told me he had a plan for a special issue, to incorporate the papers that our colleague and I were submitting. He suggested that we write a joint introduction to the other papers that would appear in the journal. To this day, I do not know if he had simply forgotten about rejecting my idea the day before or had changed his mind. Perhaps it is not important. Anyway, working together with my supervisor was a new experience. In the process of editing the special journal issue, the conventional supervisor/student relationship was more or less dissolved, replaced by a co-operative relationship in which we worked together on a common project. I learned a lot from seeing how he constructed a text and made a textual argument. When we had both read a paper together, it was interesting to see what kind of critical points he would make and compare them to the ones I would make. If I were to sum up the main points that emerged from the collaboration, they would be as follows:

1. Transformation of the supervisor-student relationship into a collaborative relationship with a focus on jointly producing a product.
2. A change from monologues about my material to dialogues about shared material.
3. Learning from seeing him work with the texts, materials, and problems we faced.
4. Enlightenment from the many informal meetings and conversations we had during the process, in which I would learn about the writers, their products, their positions in the intellectual field, and their personal stories.
5. Tuition in the form of seeing how he would evaluate texts (mine, his own, and the other writers'). In this respect, I learned indirectly about academic standards of the field, applied in an academic evaluation process.
6. During the work on the special issue, I developed a social network with other writers in the field.

Formative Apprenticeship

The above example highlights how feedback can become part of working on a shared project rather than working from a distance and giving advice on something that is not directly related to the supervisor's own work. From a more general perspective, literature on assessment typically refers to a common distinction between formative and summarizing assessment. The formative assessment is described as proactive, very much aligned with what happened in the above writing and learning while doing, whilst the summarizing assessment is said to be retroactive (Nevo, 1986).

The formative assessment is primarily an assessment practice seeking to improve and develop an activity while it is undertaken, as in the previous example that concerned collaboration on a writing and editing project. The summarizing assessment is above all a practice appraising the results of a given effort. Summarizing forms of assessment practices can also have formative aspects when influencing the student's behavior. In this respect, apprenticeship forms of assessment tend to focus on guidance and feedback in relation to proficiency in becoming part of a community of practice. In relation to doctoral training, the student is assessed on the background of her contributions to the community of practice rather than on her ability to engage in self-reflection. More precisely, the value of, for example, creativity in work processes or independent problem solving is judged by someone other than the student, in relation to the quality of her products and the professional standards of the workplace. In contrast to a focus on assessment as individual self-examination or monitoring, assessment in apprenticeship has the community of practice, its products, and the increased and intensified participation of the apprentices as its points of reference. Part of this involves increased self-government by the apprentice in the community of practice, but this independence is not seen as acquired through self-direction or self-reflection. Rather, it is made possible through a continual assessment of the apprentice's ability to gradually master the tools and acquire the knowledge of the community of practice (Tanggaard & Elmholdt, 2008). Let us now look at more examples of how this proceeds in actual doctoral training.

Thomas Is Told That His Text Has "Potential"

Here, our colleague Thomas Szulevicz tells his story of supervisory feedback on his draft dissertation and how he learned the craft of writing through intense guidance and acquiring the academic "habitus":

Four months prior to my submission date I had a meeting with my supervisor and three colleagues who, prior to the meeting, had read a 200-page draft of my dissertation (I had written a monograph). My colleagues began by giving me some very useful feedback based on their reading, but it is mainly the words of my supervisor which I remember: "Thomas, there is potential in your draft." It was a nice way of telling me that there was still a lot of work to be done before submitting the dissertation four months later. At the meeting, my supervisor also proposed a meeting once every 14 days in the following four months, which was another nice way of telling me that my work required more organization. I left the meeting with very mixed emotions. On the one hand, I was extremely frustrated. I had only four months left and I had just been (kindly) told that there was still a very long way to go. On the other hand, my supervisor had succeeded in convincing me that, with considerable effort, my goal could still be achieved.

Four months later, I submitted my dissertation and it was accepted. The episode highlights some interesting aspects relating to writing a PhD, but also to academic work in general. During the last four months of my PhD course I was forced to make a coherent product out of my data and theoretical readings and through this process, I realized what academic writing is all about. Most of all, I applied a critical approach to each and every part of my academic work and thus moved beyond banal considerations. Everything synthesized. For me, writing a PhD was a learning process in which I gradually came to terms with the academic habitus.

I also learned how important (good and engaged) supervision is. Today, in my current position as associate professor I do a lot of supervision. I always try to engage in my student's projects, I try to push them as far as possible, and I tell them when I see potential in their projects; moreover, I do not shy away from saying there is still a lot of work to be done.

Thomas seems to have had a trusting relationship with his supervisor. It may be due to this trust that he perceived the comment that his draft had "potential" as encouraging. What he was told was that it was not (yet) good enough; other students might have interpreted the message as discouraging. Furthermore, the plan to hold a meeting every fortnight could have been perceived as a lack of confidence in the student's ability to move forward at the required pace. Feedback is not encouraging or discouraging, good or bad, friendly or mean per se. Much depends on the relationship, the situation, and the student's ability to make the most of obstacles, as we found in Chapter 4. Equally, the kind of feedback students require should cover much more than writing skills and text production. Here, Charlotte's former second supervisor, Stephen Billett, reflects upon the candidate-dependent process of supervision:

Stephen Reflects on Candidate-Dependent Supervision

The central roles of higher research degree supervision is assisting candidates identify an appropriate problem, guide them in the kind of reading required to understand that problem and what ideas can be used to critically appraise it, select procedures to investigate it, and then supervise and assist in the production of a dissertation or a series of articles. In essence, it is about research training. It is these tasks, or something similar, that are usually stated in academic workload formula associated with research higher degree supervision. But inevitably it is far more than that. It is most often a very candidate-dependent process of development, which as a supervisor I constantly need to remind myself about.

For instance, the candidates I supervise are mature age adults, usually with long work histories, and very short histories of engagement with higher education, and then after long working lives. Hence, their capacities to write effectively and engage in the scale of the task presented by doctoral studies are often significant considerations. So, much of the work across the supervision period is assisting learning how to write and in particular genre. There is no easy way. It is very person dependent, in terms of their understanding of grammar, syntax, the extent and accuracy of their vocabulary, etc. Hence, a large part of the work is assisting with both the development of these capacities, but also the confidence to write effectively, and clearly. Of course, this is a task that continues across the life course. However, it presents itself as a significant challenge within a doctoral candidature. Yet, it is reasonably easy for me to be sympathetic here. I took that same journey myself many years ago and am still on it.

The candidate-dependent nature of that supervision plays out in other particular ways. For instance, most of my candidates are part-time, which means that they complete their doctoral work over a period of six years or more, while balancing work, family and their studies. A lot can happen in that time in terms of changes in their abilities, understandings and values which is central to the doctoral process, although not wholly acknowledged except in the dissertation or publications. During that journey significant changes can occur in their lives which impact upon their abilities, energies and commitments. For my candidates, these have included their partners and children becoming seriously sick, a messy divorce and crises of confidence, and even in one case the family home being cut in half by a falling tree, which caused the need to relocate and rebuild. How each of the candidates responded to these kinds of challenges is as diverse as candidates themselves and their circumstances. Moreover, how the supervisor responds cannot simply be in terms of the completion of the doctoral study, even when that is the explicit request. Instead, the role can variously include becoming a confidant, supporter, provider of assistance, and advocate for the candidate within higher education institutions whose processes are sometimes administratively adept, but lacking in appropriate responsiveness (and perhaps increasingly so). Occasionally, it is also trying to provide this kind of support which is needed, yet the candidate is resistant.

So, the obvious point to anybody who has supervised, but maybe not to candidates, is that supervision is more than processes purposefully directed towards the generation of a dissertation/series of articles; it is also about a process of learning and development, which is going to be candidate-dependent. Hence, beyond the workload descriptions is a far larger and nuanced task.

As suggested by Stephen in the above, the kinds of advice, support, encouragement, and feedback needed as part of a doctoral study vary according to the students involved as well as their preferences and life circumstances. Doctoral training is dependent on what we have termed the landscape of communities of practice, both with respect to the research task and also more broadly in other parts of the student's life. Aspects of making a living and learning in doctoral training certainly involve boundary crossing in and between various practices where different identities are negotiated (Tanggaard, 2007). This involves a focus on the horizontal aspects of learning through the participation of the doctoral student in a range of social practices where the actions of bridging, exchanging, and negotiating various demands become relevant. The context-dependent personal dimensions of supervision definitely points at how feedback during the doctoral journey cannot be conceived of as single instances delivered from supervisor to student, but must rather be seen as a continuous horizontal process involving sometimes conflicting voices and different and colliding concerns and demands, as when trying to write a paper whilst serving the needs of family members and constantly judging which activity should have priority.

Obtaining feedback seems to involve prioritizing the strange life of being a researcher and doing real research. In the following, we will examine feedback in a more specific sense. Why and how should one expose oneself to the feedback needed to get the writing going, which is so essential for disseminating ideas in the academic world?

Writing for "Real" and "Blind" Reviewers

Learning to become a researcher is very much a matter of learning to learn from feedback. This can be a tough game, even for the well-established. I, Lene, remember one of the most encouraging moments in my doctoral training was when my supervisor told me he frequently had his papers rejected. This made me confident that I would make it, as I often found the anonymous feedback from reviewers very annoying and hard to tackle. The relationship between writer and blind reviewer is addressed here by Knausgaard from the view of the blind reviewer (see Blind Review by Knausgaard box).

Knausgaard's text underlines a very important source of feedback during doctoral training, that is, peer reviews and comments from journal reviewers and editors. The option of obtaining blind reviews is becoming even more prevalent. There is a growing expectation that students publish articles while they are pursuing their degree (Lee & Kamler, 2008; Nettles & Millett, 2006). This means that the pressure to publish in peer-reviewed journals is now moving downwards *into* the doctoral process, resulting in a situation where doctoral students are expected to present papers and perform in academia while still learning the skills needed to succeed in academia. This is both a burden and an opportunity for learning, by doing something "for real." Scholarly writing is not an instrumental skill set that

Blind Review by Knausgaard

I remember once, I was in my late twenties and working for a journal and I was dealing with a contribution commissioned from an established poet. I read the poem. Then I made some comments and proposed a few changes, asking whether it would be possible to expand it a little in a certain direction. The poet's answer can be summed up in a single sentence: "Who the hell are you?" I was completely dumbfounded. My comments had been very cautiously phrased; they were, to my mind, justified. This was my usual manner of proofing texts by friends. Here, however, I wondered why an experienced and well-established poet was unable to handle the matter with a little professionalism.

In fact, it was not really a matter of the text in question. It was the fact that the comments came from an unknown, faceless person who was apparently intent on changing the work; it must have been seen as some form of attack. The impression was evidently that some young upstart of an academic had perceived something wrong and knew what had to be done to fix it. Objectively seen, I think the comments were on the right lines. But there is no such thing as "objectively seen" with respect to the written word: everything depends on who is writing and who is reading. Had this poet and I been better acquainted, had we formed an impression of each other and perhaps known more of the other's literary preferences, I think my comments would have been received differently. It may even had led to changes, though not necessarily in the direction I had in mind. (Knausgaard, 2013)

can be acquired at the beginning of the doctoral process and then applied throughout the process. It takes time: Ideas are developed and papers are written, revised, and rewritten.

"It's All About Desire"

Writing under the pressure to publish provides opportunities for writing with a real audience in mind and for obtaining feedback from real reviewers, anonymous though they may be. However, most of the literature on scholarly writing tends to emphasize problems and negative emotions. Although "desire" is mentioned, it seems relevant to further investigate those activities that may support experiences of desire, delight, and joy. One of the most encouraging books on producing text is Becker's book *Writing for Social Scientists*. Here, he questions the idea that willpower and hard work take care of everything:

It's partly sound: nothing will happen without the work. It's misleading if it leads you to think that working hard is all it takes. Many sociologists work hard but accomplish little. You must also take some chances. Let others see your work, open yourself to criticism. That may be frightening, even painful, in the short run. But the long-range consequences of not getting your work done are much more painful. (Becker, 2007, p. 174)

This is to say that we must expose ourselves to feedback that potentially includes exposing ourselves to criticism and even humiliation. Becker earns the right to insist on the simple act of publication by telling his own story of a quite painful review.

Among other things, he [the editor] said that whole sentences and paragraphs sounded like they have been translated from German, word for word. I didn't read German [...] but I knew that was bad. One memorable paragraph quoted one of our most ponderous sentences and added this commentary (given here in its entirety): "Stink! Stink! Stink!"

So, what do you do? Do you stay in bed and decide never to show any writing to anybody, ever again? What Becker did was the opposite: "[The editor's] letter strengthened my desire to write clear, understandable prose that sounded as if it had been in English all along" (Becker, 2007, p. 93). This feedback was turned into what Becker terms an "addiction to serious re-writing" (p. 93). He even finds that editing his own and other people's texts becomes more rewarding as he gets more experienced and tries out new ways of challenging himself to write more clearly; eventually he even finds entertainment in using fictional and visual sources of inspiration. Rewriting becomes a pleasurable pursuit.

The Necessity of Untidy Texts

A text can never be written in one shot. Writing is a form of thinking (Becker, 2007); an investigation (Richardson, 2003); and a way to involve oneself in dialogue with others (Van Maanen, 2010), with theories, and with data (Alvesson & Kärreman, 2011). Jane Speedy (2012), who will reappear in the role of supervisor in Chapter 8, argues that all writing spaces accumulate stories and people brought into the writing process by the writer. As noted by Van Maanen (2010, pp. 243–244):

The social and contextual aspects of writing include reading other writers, discussing our ideas of content and style with colleagues, the various shaping roles that are played by co-authors, critics, reviewers, readers, friends, relatives, (dreaded) thesis advisors both present and past, and the writing to and for others in a language whose grammar, tone, voice, genre, and figures of speech literally encode collectivity.

As writers, we are constantly in dialogue with material or speculative others (Pineau, 2012) as we—through writing—get into dialogue with our own concepts, investigate socially learned categories, and explore how to think otherwise (St. Pierre, 1997). From these perspectives it becomes evident that it is counterproductive to aim for a "perfect" text from the outset. Elbow (2007) shows how personal writing can remove the focus from a perceived, perfect end result and let the writer experiment and write more freely. Similarly, within health care research, Ellingson (2006) has suggested that the erasure of researchers' bodies obscures the complexities of knowledge production resulting in "tidy" accounts. We assume that these neat pieces she refers to might be the result of what Elbow (1981, p. xix) terms "defensive writing," as addressed in Chapter 3.

When we invest our experiences or thoughts-in-progress in our writing, we increase the risk of producing untidy texts; however, we might also decrease the risk of being boring (or bored) and in addition learn something new in the process. According to Richardson (1990, p. 49), such papers might be academically insignificant but literarily significant because this process helps one find a frame in which to write and experiment with tone, narrative stance, metaphors, and audience. Some of these untidy texts or writings-in-progress may even find their way to publication.

An Untidy Text or "How a Detour Became a Highway"

Our experience is that lots of students (and even experienced scientists) struggle even harder to analyze, categorize, and order. Becker (2007, p. 134) states it this way: "What if we cannot, just *cannot*, make order out of the chaos? I don't know about other people, but beginning a new paper gives me anxiety's classical physical symptoms." One supposedly anxiety-reducing strategy is to try to tidy up to be able to write a tidy text! This strategy can, however, turn out to be unproductive, demotivating, and even restrictive of creativity. Instead, another strategy is to write untidy texts. A supposed writing detour might turn into a highway. The following untidy text was produced during Charlotte's doctoral journey at a time when she was almost drowning in data, struggling to find an analytical strategy and at the same time feeling an urge to produce and think through writing. What do you do when you feel that writing is your lifeline, but you have nothing trustworthy to write about? Here is an account of Charlotte's highly chaotic interaction with data:

Days pass at the research retreat. I create five main categories, subdividing these so as to include much of my data. Yet somehow, I find the categories boring.

They do not really tell me anything new. I start over by identifying significant incidents (or at least incidents which seem to be significant) and transfer them onto individual sheets of paper, giving each sheet a headline. I continue with this "project" for about two days until I realise that the individual sheets are way too small, and that my notes are so reduced that I cannot remember what social situations they were parts of.

I print out my interview transcripts and digital field notes and ask the retreat manager for scissors. I cut up every so-called unit of meaning and put them into individual piles, coding them for emotions, activities, place, the interviewees' job description . . . creating headlines along the way. There is now a narrow walking path from my bed to the door of my room. Phineas remains mute, lying within Byatt's novel at the bottom of my suitcase. I go for a long walk by the sea.

This disclosure of chaos was later published as part of a methodological paper in a special issue on collaborative writing as method of inquiry. The key theme of the paper was how to find a dialogue partner—that is, to get feedback—when you are all alone. Eventually, the paper came to unsettle the notion of categorization and proposed a narrative strategy in dialogue with the fictional protagonist, Phineas, from the novel *The Biographer's Tale* (Byatt, 2001). The fictional character, Phineas who "remains mute" in the above quote is brought to life and turned into a dialogue partner in writing. The published article (Wegener, 2014) explains how the expected analytical process of identifying categories failed because it was detached from subjective experiences and values. The article tells the story of how the anticipated "neat categorisation" never emerged. However, these methodological reflections would never have turned into a publishable text without dialogue with the editors of the publishing journal who had initially accepted an abstract.

Precious Feedback From Editors

Charlotte had pieces of writing like the one quoted above, but the text was not coming together. The feedback process started at deadline with an exhausted and embarrassed author:

From: Charlotte Wegener

Sent: 01 March 2013 12:18

To: Jonathan Wyatt

Subject: RE: Drafts for special issue of CSCM

Hi Jonathan

It is very embarrassing but the manuscript "A collaborative writing strategy when you are alone" is not as I hoped it to be right now. Parts of the paper are ready while other parts need some clear thinking. Contents and structure are almost there and you can have it as it is, but it lacks flow and coherence. I can send it or revise it as you please.

Sorry for the inconvenience it may cause.

Best regards
Charlotte

From: Jonathan Wyatt

Sent: 1. marts 2013 13:49

To: Charlotte Wegener

Cc: Ken Gale

Subject: RE: Drafts for special issue of CSCM

No worries, Charlotte. Take some time to get it into a shape you're more happy with. One week? Two? More? Let us know what's realistic for you and we'll try to work around it.

Jonathan

So far, so good. The writer gained some time but still has no idea about how to become "happier" with the text. Two weeks later, however, she had to reveal what she had and had not accomplished. She knew she had to follow Becker's advice and get the text out the door:

From: Charlotte Wegener

Sent: 16 March 2013 13:07

To: Jonathan Wyatt

Cc: Ken Gale

Subject: RE: Drafts for special issue of CSCM

Dear Jonathan and Ken

Now the draft is better than two weeks ago. There is still work to be done, I know. I hope that you find it to be worthy of further development and I am confident that reviews will help me to take the next steps.

Thank you for your patience.

Best regards
Charlotte

It turned out to be wise to ask for feedback and not spend more time on introspective struggle, although the editors had opened the door to this possibility. What they turned out to be capable of doing—just like Thomas's supervisor—was to spot the potential of the text. What they also did was to give tangible advice about how to make this potential unfold. They also proposed literature that might inspire this kind of writing, which made the advice even more grounded:

From: Jonathan Wyatt

Sent: 22. marts 2013 16:51

To: Charlotte Wegener

Subject: Drafts for special issue of CSCM

Dear Charlotte,

We've now had a chance to read your paper. Thanks so much for sending it.

You write well and engagingly, and there's much that we like about this paper—the premise itself, the way in which you flow between places and between areas of reflection and focus; and we have a strong sense of your presence on the page, working it out, working at the challenges you're facing.

We have two areas for you to consider. Firstly, it's our experience that the paper is not yet sufficiently addressing collaborative writing as method of inquiry. You only refer to it towards the end of the paper and even there it feels underplayed, given the theme of the issue. (See our comments on this on the attached).

Our suggestion is that you might use AS Byatt as a character, a voice, with whom you converse as the paper progresses. And/or use Phineas in the same way—there could be a three-way conversation running through the paper.

Given the strong literary feel to your writing, we feel confident that you could make such a device work—but you may have other ideas. The key point is that you need to find a way to foreground collaborative writing as method of inquiry, because as it stands it's more a paper about working with and against traditional qualitative research methodology—which you do well but it's been done before.

You'll see that we suggest you have a look at Jane Speedy's and Elyse Pineau's papers in the latest issue of *International Review of Qualitative Research*, because each writes—differently—about collaborative writing while writing alone. Let us know if you need us to send you a PDF.

We also make some suggestions on the attached for how you might broaden your critique of post positivist approaches to qualitative inquiry (e.g., looking at St Pierre's work on "data").

Does what we're suggesting make sense? We intend our feedback to be positive and encouraging—we'd very much like a revised version of your paper in the issue. What do you think?

Please get back to us if there's anything we've said that needs clarifying or elaborating.

Best wishes,
Jonathan and Ken

What the editors do is one of the keys to effective feedback. They are looking for what is there and how to unlock the potential. They acknowledge the literary feel of the writing as a basis for their suggestion to rewrite parts of the text in an even more literary form—a dialogue. They also explain why this may be the way to move forward, that is, the paper has to address collaborative writing more explicitly. While the author's original idea was inspired significantly by the call for this special issue, she almost forgot this idea during her struggle and given the increasing pressure of the deadline. Feedback was needed to get the writing back on track, and it was not difficult to make the suggested device work. All of this points at the circularity of knowing.

The Circularity of Knowing

We can be encouraged to involve in dialogue and expose ourselves and our texts to other's reactions by Weick's reversal of some ideas about causality that are often taken for granted. Take a look at this appreciation of Weick in the words of Gioia (2006), who highlights the idea of being an explorer. Here, he elaborates on what he terms Weick's "recipe" for sense making:

Weick's "Recipe" for Sense Making

How can I know what I think until I see what I say? What a wonderful turn of phrase. Now, Weick is not the first to articulate the essential idea here. Schutz's (1967) treatise argued that people can only know what they are doing (actually, have been doing) after they have done it. Bateson (1972: xvi, cited by Wick 1979) noted that "an explorer can never know what he is exploring until it has been explored." Wiener (cited by Bennis 2003) made a similar observation when he said, "I never know what I say until I hear the response" (which is an interesting variant on the same idea). [...] The consequences of developing this line of thought are not trivial. It even leads to further non-obvious, but demonstrably defensible conclusions that goals are often formed *after* action (as a kind of retrospective explanation for what people think they must have been doing). (Gioia, 2006, p. 1713–1714)

What is addressed here might be termed *feedback from life itself.* This presupposes, obviously, that you are involved in life—not least in academic life. Here, our colleague Vlad Glaveanu provides two narratives about how he was encouraged to involve himself in academic life during his doctoral studies.

Vlad's Reading Group

One defining moment in my own doctoral work relates to when my supervisor initiated a reading group for her group of PhD students. We were supposed to choose a text to read each time and then come and discuss it once every two weeks. Although we didn't really have many sessions (due to all sorts of scheduling issues), the two or three times we met changed my understanding of what became an important piece of theory for my doctoral work. Since we discussed a psychology classic (Dewey's *Art as Experience*) it was initially difficult for me to "get into" the language or framing of the issue on my own. I remember that while reading this on my own I was puzzled about how to make sense of it in terms of my own research. One thing that my supervisor initiated and helped me a lot in understanding the text was to start by contextualising it within both historical time and the trajectory of the author. Our group discussion was focused not only on clarifying the meaning of certain key passages but, most of all, on making connections with both (past and present) theory and practice. This episode really showed me (once more) that doctoral work is really all about dialogue and exchange and the myth of the lone PhD student is, well, a myth!

Vlad's PhD Seminar

In my University we had a weekly PhD seminar that brought together all the students to discuss issues relevant for all or to present work in progress. This seminar was organised differently for first year PhD students because in this case the focus was on introducing them to the initial steps of this journey and preparing them for the first big assignments in the programme (the literature review, the first empirical chapter, etc.). Second and third year PhDs would meet to discuss fieldwork, data analysis and present their research. This was an extremely fruitful exercise. I remember being asked to prepare different types of presentations of my research, including a 2 min "elevator brief" (how would you describe your research to someone in a couple of minutes in the elevator?) or, my favourites, "how would you describe what you are doing for the press?" and "what about for your grandmother?" These seemed like games at the time but they actually helped me and my colleagues clarify what is the core of our theses and how we can become more effective in presenting our ideas to others. Another useful exercise involved having a colleague present your project to others (after discussing it with you). It was great to see not only how others understand your work but to actually notice new things within your own research! In the end Bakhtin was right to say that we need others because we can't see the back of our own head or, in this case, the multiple sides of one's own doctoral project.

As Vlad is emphasizing here, realizing that you are not alone as a PhD student and that others and their voices are needed to make it through the whole process brilliantly underlines the importance of getting feedback from the broader audience that is part of one's life and the research community. The following story illustrates how Charlotte learned this the hard way in her own process.

"People Think by Acting"

Charlotte's First Conference

The first time I went to a conference, I assumed that the only format was a sole-authored paper and thus 20 minutes of solo-performance combined with 10 minutes of responding to—hopefully kind—questions. I need not dwell on my experiences of stress and concern until my presentation session was over. I learned a lot, however; I would have preferred a flatter learning curve if my prior anticipation had been a little more pleasurable. A co-authored and co-presented paper, a poster, or a round table presentation of work in progress might have been more helpful for a novice conference participant.

This is not to discourage anyone from composing a sole-authored conference paper or approaching the podium alone. Rather, the aim here is to point to other, more social and dialogue-oriented strategies for conference participation and for learning in general. The dissertation is a sole-authored product (for an exception, see Gale, Speedy, & Wyatt, 2010), but the production process does not need to be either solitary or lonely. Most advice about conference participation consists of idealistic tips for preparation such as read the abstracts (if available), check out professors you would like to connect with, and so on. Our strategy here is more in line with the overall philosophy of the book: You need to explore the landscape while being there. This means that you cannot know what to do until you experience the response to your actions. To attend a conference with an apprentice state of mind is first and foremost a willingness to be present and to act. The only way to prepare for that is to practice your agility and courage in a general sense. Following Dewey, you need to act in the world in order to experience what happens. It may look like this. Actually, it did look precisely like this.

Looking for a Second Supervisor

After my solo presentation of my solely authored paper, exhausted and exhilarated, I (Charlotte) seek out the professor I have been looking forward to encountering. I have read her articles and I expect to use some of her concepts to move on with my analyses. She did actually attend this session so I feel very lucky, although my self-awareness tells me that she is not there on account of my presentation. Rather is it due to the previous presenter, a well-known professor in the field of workplace learning and vocational training, Stephen Billett, whose work I do not know well. I was worried (read "scared to death") when I realized that his presentation was scheduled prior to mine. His presentation was interesting (as far as I was able to pay attention), and the connection to my research theme was obvious. However, I have a plan and I have to act now to make it happen. I have to talk to the attending professor now that she is actually in this room. I present myself to my chosen networking victim and tell her that I am pleased to meet her and that I am planning a stay abroad as part of my doctoral study. She is very kind and tells me that she enjoyed my presentation and that she knows my supervisor—is she here? How is she doing? She is fine, I reply, but I feel my courage disappear. A few exchanges and more "say hi to Lene," and she is off.

Still high on "presentation endorphins," I force my way through the crowd and say hello to Stephen Billett, the professor who presented before me. I like his ideas, I tell him and ask breathlessly if it would be possible to visit his research group. He is busy right now he tells me, but he will be back. Not high on anything anymore I return from this gruelling climb to the base camp; have a drink with my doctoral peers and go to bed very early after having shot my first selfie ever—me with a blank stare holding a sign saying "no smoking in bed." This sign is weirdly liberating to me. Finally a "no" I can accept without regrets. Networking at conferences is over-estimated, I tell myself before I sleep—or maybe I just don't possess the skills. The next day, however, Stephen Billett does actually come back as promised. I am very welcome to visit, he tells me and spends some five minutes advising me about the next steps to take and some of his work that I might benefit from reading, and then he is off. I forward the information he asked for as soon as I get back home, and he replies immediately. One year later, I board a plane with a suitcase full of writing projects, questions and feeling adventurous.

Retrospective Preparation?

We might label this way of going to conferences as "retrospective preparation." Or "navigating the landscapes of (im)possibilities." The strategy narrated here—and it can indeed be questioned whether it deserves to be termed a *strategy*—is meant only as a provocative opening to the discussion. Preparation is a virtue that we do not wish to belittle. Equally, so is perseverance. Without hard work and even stubbornness, significant amounts of empirical data and hundreds of others peoples' articles and books will never turn into completed papers and dissertations. Both preparation and perseverance are crucial in academic work for both doctoral students and experienced professors, but the doctoral student in this narrative performs poorly within these parameters. What we want to stress, however, is that these virtues must be balanced. Most doctoral students do not suffer from "scratching the surface" or "easygoing" strategies. Rather, meticulousness and workaholic behavior seems to torment academics. It may feel like safe behavior ("if I work more, I will get more work done"; "if I stick to my plan, I will not waste time"), but unfortunately this is not the fact if we look into doctoral drop-out statistics. Meticulous preparation and hard work in itself does not guarantee great results. It might even make us more vulnerable to feedback. Rather, we advocate *adequate* preparation combined with agility and a curious and unpretentious "I am here to learn" rather than "'I am here to impress" attitude.

Learning From Giving Feedback

"I am here to learn" rather than "I am here to impress" is also a useful strategy when *giving* feedback. Learning to give effective feedback as a doctoral student is relevant in peer groups, at doctoral training classes and conferences, and eventually when invited to write a book review or be a blind reviewer of a manuscript. Although these activities are time-consuming, they extend the student's network of relationships and serve as opportunities for practicing the feedback culture of academia. If the driving force, however, is to impress, giving feedback does not serve well as a learning resource and may be both anxiety provoking for the student and unhelpful for the one receiving the feedback. We can be encouraged to adopt a learning attitude to giving feedback by Becker (2007), who tells the story of how he learned in this way:

> Rosanna Hertz, now a colleague but then a very advanced student, came into my office one day and said she'd like to talk to me about a chapter of her thesis-in-progress, which I had edited for her [...], she didn't quite understand the principles that governed what I had done. Could I go over the document with

her and explain them? I told her that I wasn't sure what principles governed my editorial judgement [...]. But I agreed to do my best. I wondered whether I actually did follow any general principles of editing and thought that, if I did, I might discover them by trying to explain them to her. (Becker, 2007, p. 26)

Just as Paré (2010) found, Becker's feedback is potentially useful but he does not explicitly refer to the rules and rhetoric of the discipline—the "general principles." Luckily, this student asks for explanations and thus initiates a learning process for both of them. The rules and rhetoric of the discipline becomes a theme of discussion, which enables her to make her own judgments about writing style. Being forced to explain and become involved in dialogues with students in his writing classes and with colleagues provides him with ever more material. Wagner (2010, p. 39) explains Becker's strategy as the iterative process of building knowledge though feedback in this way: "Becker revised some more, read some more, wrote some more, and talked some more. As his teaching and research exchanges with other colleagues and students moved forward, he began organising materials for the book and eventually showed it to a publisher." Becker already had a long career of researching, writing, and supervising. Giving and receiving feedback is an opportunity for learning no matter how experienced you are.

Good Advice for the PhD Student

- Think of feedback as a key driver for learning throughout a research career.
- Ask explicitly for the feedback you need at specific times.
- Be open to unwanted feedback—it might widen your horizons.
- When the feedback hurts, talk it over with someone you trust and who is able to decode its potential. Just like your own writings, the potential of the feedback may need to be unlocked.
- During formal sessions of oral feedback (at tutorials, conferences, and doctoral training courses) ask if you can audio record or arrange in advance with someone else to take notes.
- Always carry a notebook or your cell phone for when life provides feedback. A few words, some scribbles, or a photo are often enough to assist memory.
- Give the kind of feedback you feel capable of and regard it as an opportunity for socialization, not to show off.

Good Advice for the Supervisor

- Think of feedback as a walk with the student—an opportunity for pointing out discoveries made; battles fought; and what seem to be new, hip destinations.

- Writing is identity work and feedback always involves identity issues—make this explicit.
- Use collaborative feedback opportunities in supervision groups with your PhD students.
- Realize that you may not be very good at giving feedback and compensate by creating common work projects where you get feedback from others and learn together with students.
- Use creative practices as they do at London School of Economics, re-told in Vlad's story above. Let students present their peers' projects; use elevator pitches; and turn things upside down to create wider feedback opportunities.

Conclusion

In this chapter, we have discussed feedback and the craft of asking for, benefitting from, and giving it. We have shown different options for dialogue and ways to obtain others' reactions to our work. Feedback involves exposure to criticism. Nevertheless, feedback is a crucial source for moving forward and should not be postponed until we feel that our thoughts or our texts are finished. Based on Weick and others, we have illustrated that we can know what we are doing only after we have done it, that is, after we have experienced other people's reactions to our work. Getting feedback from a broader audience and learning to give appreciative feedback ourselves are part of research life and keys to deep involvement in the research community.

References

Alvesson, M., & Kärreman, D. (2011). *Qualitative research and theory development: Mystery as method*. Los Angeles: Sage.

Becker, H. S. (2007). *Writing for social scientists: How to start and finish your thesis, book, or article*. London: University of Chicago Press.

Byatt, A. S. (2001). *The biographer's tale*. New York: Vintage Books.

Elbow, P. (1981). *Writing with power: Techniques for mastering the writing process*. New York: Oxford University Press.

Elbow, P. (2007). Voice in writing again: Embracing contraries. *College English, 70*(2), 168–188.

Ellingson, L. L. (2006). Embodied knowledge: Writing researchers' bodies into qualitative health research. *Qualitative Health Research, 16*(2), 298–310.

Gale, K., Speedy, J., & Wyatt, J. (2010). Gatecrashing the oasis? A joint doctoral dissertation play. *Qualitative Inquiry, 16*(1), 21–28.

Gioia, D. A. (2006). On Weick: An appreciation. *Organization Studies, 27*(11), 1709.

Knausgaard, K. O. (2013). *Sjælens Amerika.* Copenhagen: Lindhardt & Ringhof.

Lave, J., & Wenger, E. (1991). *Situated learning: Legitimate peripheral participation.* Cambridge: Cambridge University Press.

Lee, A., & Kamler, B. (2008). Bringing pedagogy to doctoral publishing. *Teaching in Higher Education, 13*(5), 511–523.

Nettles, M. T., & Millett, C. M. (2006). *Three magic letters: Getting to Ph.D.* Baltimore, MD: Johns Hopkins University Press.

Nevo, D. (1986). The conceptualisation of educational evaluation: An analytical review of the literature. In E. R. House (Ed.), *New directions in educational evaluation* (pp. 15–29). London: Falmer Press.

Noe, R. A., Clarke, A. D. M., & Klein, H. J. (2014). Learning in the twenty-first century workplace. *Annual Review of Organizational Psychology and Organizational Behavior, 1*, 245–275.

Paré, A. (2010). Making sense of supervision: Deciphering feedback. In P. Thomson & M. Walker (Eds.), *The Routledge doctoral student's companion: Getting to grips with research in education and the social sciences* (pp. 107–115). London: Routledge.

Pineau, E. (2012). Haunted by ghosts: Collaborating with absent others. *International Review of Qualitative Research, 5*(4), 459–465.

Richardson, L. (1990). *Writing strategies: Reaching diverse audiences.* Newbury Park, CA: Sage.

Richardson, L. (2003). Writing: A method of inquiry. In N. K. Denzin & Y. S. Lincoln (Eds.), *Collecting and interpreting qualitative materials* (2nd ed., pp. 499–541). Thousand Oaks, CA: Sage.

Speedy, J. (2012). Collaborative writing and ethical know-how: Movements within the space around scholarship, the academy and the social research imaginary. *International Review of Qualitative Research, 5*(4), 349–356.

St. Pierre, E. A. (1997). Circling the text: Nomadic writing practices. *Qualitative Inquiry, 3*(4), 403–417.

Tanggaard, L. (2007). Boundary crossing between school and work. *Journal of Education and Work, 20*(5), 453–466.

Tanggaard, L. & Elmholdt, E. (2008). Assessment in practice: An inspiration from apprenticeship. I: *Scandinavian Journal of Educational Research, 52*(1), 97–116.

Van Maanen, J. (2010). A song for my supper. More tales of the field. *Organizational Research Methods, 13*(2), 240–255.

Wagner, J. (2010). Ignorance in educational research: How not knowing shapes new knowledge. In P. Thomson & M. Walker (Eds.), *The Routledge doctoral student's companion: Getting to grips with research in education and social sciences* (pp. 31–42). London: Routledge.

Wegener, C. (2014). Writing with Phineas: How a fictional character from A. S. Byatt helped me turn my ethnographic data into a research text. *Cultural Studies—Critical Methodologies, 14*(4), 351–360.

Chapter Eight

"Get a Life" or Simply "Live Your Life"

Abstract

Purpose: This chapter discusses questions related to academic life and identity during and beyond the doctoral studies. It addresses how apprenticeship relations continue, change, and end.

Central message: Learning to become a researcher cannot be considered a disinterested, neutral, and nonpersonal process. We are always developing as persons along the journey of becoming researchers.

Takeaways: It is pertinent during the research education to spend time considering what might happen after the study and how one can begin to plan a career during the PhD studies. Learning and identity formation as a researcher is a life-long process.

Keywords: Researcher identity, the doctoral journey, start before you are ready, entering the scene, finding the middle, trajectories of participation, abandoning the rules, stepping stones.

Putting an End to Uncertainty?

At the end of the peer group session described in Chapter 5, Charlotte complains: "It is anxiety-provoking to try and finish my dissertation, because I don't know if I can. I'm afraid that I cannot put an end to uncertainty. I'm afraid that I will never be able to finish." On a practical level, this kind of anxiety is tied to the intense, final sprint of writing the dissertation. Yet "putting an end to uncertainty" addresses epistemological issues far beyond finishing a dissertation. Wisely, peer group member Ninna, who recently passed her oral defense, reassures Charlotte: "I am still working with unfinished thoughts, and my writing is still in progress. I had hoped for a better feeling of closure. But, is this because my dissertation was not good enough? No, because the examiners said it was good enough." And this is merely what research is like: a never-ending and developing process (Wegener, Meier, & Ingerslev, 2014, p. 10).

Finishing the dissertation obviously does not put an end to uncertainty. This chapter discusses questions related to academic life and identity during and beyond the doctoral studies. In which ways may apprenticeship relationships continue, change, and end? How do we chart desired areas of future research life and make them feasible to reach? Questions of how to live a life as a researcher are relevant throughout the doctoral journey. We examine how we as researchers can mine our lives for inspiration, and what we can do in order to refuel and maintain the spirit. We also examine how, as a supervisor, helping your students plan for the future requires consideration as to whether the research life is a good fit for the student, and ways of inviting the student into the wider research community, as well as advice about other career possibilities. A doctoral study is not something to get done with before we can "get a life."

Moving Fast or Learning to Live a Researcher's Life?

Questions of getting a life or learning to live a life as a researcher are often tackled in instrumental terms, as a matter of setting goals and moving fast. Many textbooks with advice in relation to doctoral training are based on the premise that writing faster and finishing quickly is a matter of acquiring new habits, as when students are advised to spend at least 15 minutes each day on their dissertation (James & Slater, 2014, p. 5). "We believe that you can finish your dissertation faster without sacrificing quality, but it's not likely to be easy. You will be up against several challenges. In our experience, some of the biggest obstacles include maintaining focus and persistence to reach your ultimate goal, finishing your research" (James & Slater, 2014, p. xix).

There will be challenges, and in this book we address how these can be tackled not only as tremendous obstacles facing each individual, and with goal setting as the ultimate solution, but as something larger that is dealt with in the communities of research at large.

Learning involves our lives, and dealing with our lives, even if we at times seem to act as if writing the next paper or finishing our dissertation will not demand too much energy or engagement from our side. The reality is that 15-minute recipes are mostly made up of dreams, and in fact, working on one's dissertation can cause quite of lot of (fun) trouble.

In Search of a Researcher Identity

From the apprenticeship perspective, the learning involved in becoming a researcher cannot merely be considered a disinterested, neutral, and nonpersonal process. In the process of learning, we are always developing as persons. From this perspective, cognition "is a complex social phenomenon . . . distributed—stretched over, not divided among—mind, body, activity and culturally organized settings (which include other actors)" (Lave, 1988, p. 1). And learning is "an integral part of generative social practice in the lived-in world" (Lave & Wenger, 1991, p. 35). Packer and Goicoechea (2000) claim that to come to know or learn something is rarely an end in itself highly removed from everyday practice. The search for identity, for belonging, and to be a part of something is what gets people to "participate in communities of practice in many different ways (Greeno & The Middle School Mathematics Through Applications Project Group, 1998, p. 10), and this participation structures the learning opportunities and barriers.

The Purpose of Learning

Dreier (2008) clarifies the situative perspective by claiming that when we learn in one place, in one or more communities of practice, we are in the process of developing our potential to participate in a more competent, stronger, and more full-fledged way in other places. The purpose of learning is often simply to prepare us for another practice, such as the life after our time as research students. When we encounter problems with our learning, it is because we cannot engage more intensively in the practice where we are seeking to capture learning. Other times, we tend to develop a learning identity that is in conflict with the institutional perceptions of what is the important learning in the particular practice within which we are taking part. For a research student, problems with learning can arise when we are, for example, having a hard time seeing ourselves as part of the research life, when receiving harsh criticism or feedback, or when networking does not work, as described in the previous chapter.

The Total Life

The learning process around a PhD study can play out within, and is dependent of, connections or conflicts between many different practices. Holzkamp (1998) emphasized, from a critical psychological perspective, this point in relation to conflictual participation. As a university-employed educator and researcher, he attempted for a while to create reading and study groups, where he, together with the students, could discuss texts. He quickly noticed that very few would participate. And while at first he was disappointed by the lack of engagement, he later realized, from speaking with his students, that many of them, either because of children or commutes, could not find the time for the study groups. Their total life collided with the good initiative, and it is important, as pointed out by Holzkamp, not to see this as a lack of intrinsic motivation. Rather, real conflicts may arise in terms of composing a complete life during a time when university life becomes a central focus of the student life. Holzkamp regrets that this conflict does not attract more discussion during instruction, counseling, and courses. We run the risk of privatizing the students' possible motivational problems, when we should instead discuss how to balance university life with the other parts of a student life.

Goal Setting as a Mutual Responsibility

Likewise, we intend to argue that learning in relation to the doctoral training is extended in time and place, and for that treason it is pertinent during the research education to spend time considering what might happen after the study, and how the student already during the PhD studies can begin to plan his or her career. It is not simply a question of the individual student setting his/her individual goals. It is a mutual responsibility in the research community to reflect on how ideas about the future can and should shape the current learning environment. This may influence strategies for publishing, the selection of research institutions, training opportunities, and more. Supervisors have, overall, considerable impact on how the individual research student develops a style and perception about what should happen after his or her training as a researcher.

Kundera on Slowness

When in need of alternative options to "moving fast" strategies and in search of a more poetic treatment of time and space, it might be worth reading Milan Kundera, the Czech author. In his novel *Immortality* (1999), he writes how a main route (*une route*) is only a line connecting two points, while a side road (*un chemin*) is a celebration of the space that it moves through. In the world of side roads, beauty is uninterrupted and forever changing. Kundera also celebrates the unexpected joys of the meandering road, which requires one to slow down. In *Slowness: A Novel* (Kundera & Asher, 1997) he describes the connection between slowness and memory, and between speed and forgetfulness. Our time, he says, is obsessed with the desire for oblivion, and it is in search of this desire that we fall captive to the demons of speed. Kundera's support for slowness is not just in support of imagination and the vision of future. It is also a support for an embodied and embedded memory that is otherwise impossible in the flight of speed. The novel is quickly read but can be digested slowly!

Always in the Middle

In many ways, finding a life as a researcher and facing the challenges and fun involved is a continuous process extended in time and space. The identity as a researcher is established through many kinds of identifications—with the research methods that you use, the community of which you are part, your peers, the papers and the texts you write, the lectures or performances given, and so on.

In his book *Identity*, Brinkmann emphasizes how identity is "a person's reflexive self-interpretation of his personal biography" (Brinkmann, 2008, p. 22). It is, in other words, a kind of self-interpretation, which people engage in, and which is about their sense of belonging. As another psychologist has put it, it is about the identity of the subjective experience that one belongs to certain places. Brinkmann also says that identity is a skill—a skill to maintain a certain narrative. Identity is the ability to maintain a special narrative about who we are, and whom we would like to be. Identity and identity narratives are precisely woven in time—from the past, which we always carry with us; to the present we live in; and to the future about which we have notions—notions that eventually structure who we are here and now.

Entering the Scene

What is it, then, that makes it worthwhile to become a researcher and identify with a research identity? Well, this identity is, first and foremost, not created in a vacuum. As Alasdair MacIntyre wrote so elegantly: "We enter upon a stage we did not design and we find ourselves part of an action that was not of our making" (MacIntyre, 1985, p. 213). It is then on this scene that we have to take responsibility for and maintain our identity narrative. At the same time, we remain a part of other scenes in addition to the one where we are currently playing.

We will propose that getting a life as a researcher involves not only becoming a member of a research community, not only constructing knowledge at various levels of expertise as a participant, but also taking a stand on the culture of one's community, in an effort to take up and overcome the estrangement and division that are consequences of participation. Learning entails both personal and social transformation and decisions regarding what kinds of activities one wants to engage in as part of doctoral training. This is not merely a trivial issue of getting a life and enjoying it, as if it was secondary to doing one's research. It is the thing. As Kirshner and Whitson (1997) pointed out, situated cognition questions the "individualist and dualist . . . commonsense assumptions about thinking and being" (p. 2). It seeks to dispense with "the Cartesian dualism of our intellectual tradition" (Kirshner & Whitson, 1997, p. 26). When our book carries the subtitle *Traveling the Landscape of Research*, we mean it, not as something that will make your life easier as a doctoral student but because taking a stance in relation to how one wants to live a life is a vital part of learning and the research process as a whole.

Progressing Along Trajectories of Participation

From our perspective, learning to become a researcher involves the continuous construction of identities and in line with the apprenticeship perspective that "one way to think of learning is as the historical production, transformation, and change of persons" (Lave & Wenger, 1991, pp. 51–52). Learning and development can be viewed as a progression along trajectories of participation and the growth of identity. It is in these practices that students develop patterns of participation that can contribute to their identities as researchers (p. 9). Here, the helpful editors whom we celebrated in Chapter 7, Jonathan Wyatt and Ken Gale, recall their encounter with the doctoral program as well as their future supervisor—an encounter which inspired them to undertake their doctoral dissertation together (Gale et al., 2010). While doing so, they address the question of identity, memory, and the present. As Gale writes concludingly in the following dual account: "Something happened and keeps on happening."

Something Keeps on Happening for Jonathan and Ken

Jonathan: Here's a moment. It doesn't relate to the dissertation itself, nor to Ken. Not directly, though it does in the end.

The moment I have in mind took place during the taught part of our doctoral programme, the Doctor of Education (Narrative and Life Story Research). Our programme director was Jane Speedy. There were eight taught "units" before the dissertation. I did one unit a term (three a year) so it took about two and a half years to complete that part of the programme, before Ken and I embarked on the dissertation.

Students travelled to Bristol for each unit and they lasted two and a half days, Thursday through to Saturday lunchtime. I loved those stages of the doctorate and the routines that evolved: driving west from Oxford along the M4, staying with friends in Bristol, walking or cycling into the university each morning. I enjoyed the rich, vibrant, stimulating days. Ken was there each time, amongst a group of us who were heading through the programme at a similar pace. It was good to be part of something.

After each unit we wrote an assignment. The second unit, in the Spring of 2004, was "Auto-ethno-graphy." We read and discussed Carolyn Ellis, Ron Pelias, Laurel Richardson, Carol Rambo Ronai, Andrew Sparkes, and others. The assignment task for each unit was open; the exact wording escapes me but there was permission for us pursue an area of our interest, to pick up on ideas from the readings and the teaching days and write an assignment of our choosing. (At least, that was the freedom I felt I had. Now, as an academic, I am writing assignment tasks and assessment criteria and know how "tight" these have to be to get approval from Boards of Studies and the like, but my experience as a student—which stayed throughout my doctoral experience—was a sense of freedom and of being trusted.)

I wrote about the loss of my father the year before. I worked on it through the early summer, then sent it to Jane as a draft. I didn't hear back for a week or so, so sent her a prompt. And another. Then another. After some weeks, I had run out of hope that I'd hear (I got used to Jane's email "habits" in due course) when her response arrived in my inbox: a long, unedited (again, typically Jane . . .) letter that told the story of her reading the essay, and reading it again.

That was the moment. It was a moment when I understood that I could do this. I could write.

There were many other, equally significant, moments that followed: Ken's suggestion that we write an assignment together, travelling together to the International Congress of Qualitative Inquiry, reading our work to an audience at a conference in Bristol, and more. And with us, all the time, Jane. Giving us permission, challenging us, and, behind the scenes, making it all possible. This first moment, where Jane seemed to notice something that I hadn't seen, seemed to unlock a door, the first door.

Jonathan Wyatt

12 January 2014

Ken: Jonathan sends this writing to me. It is always exciting and almost always a joy to receive an e-mail from him. The experience reminds me of receiving letters: sensing the materiality of the paper, noticing the postmark and the anticipation, almost the fervour, involved in ripping open the envelope. It is like that. It is to do with affect.

Our exchanges don't feel so frequent now but affect lives on a plane of immanence and is always shifting, transmutating, flowing in, moving out, and in this we are always "Good to go."[1] Since the moment of our first writing our movement in the writing has never been consistent and always been there, as Virginia Woolf so tellingly shows in the phrase, "The pen gets on the scent" (1985, p. 93). In our collaborations sometime the scent is pungent, stingingly hot and easy to follow and, at other times, it is nascent, teasingly mercurial, and tantalisingly present like the "compact of unctuous vapour" in Milton's "bogs and mires" (1960, p. 61).

And so, with this little piece of writing, I excitedly opened the envelope and began to read, quickly at first, to get the gist, my enthusiasm for the reading running away with me and then, again, in a more measured way, slowly, digesting, allowing the affect to take me, going with the flow and, with that movement, new moments of energy, allowing memory to emerge in the delicate touching of collaborative frisson.

There is such richness in those moments which I now return to and return again as I read and re-read in preparation for this writing. This plane of affect is constituted by people, Jonathan, of course, Clifford, Christine, Francine and Jane. Jane . . . Jane . . . . It is constituted by sense, a sense of these others, with whom I increasingly share this space, becoming friends, faciality, smell, a smile perhaps and always a funny look. It is constituted through the construction of memory, the emergence of sentiment, a feeling of fondness for a time that is passed and that is now, albeit briefly perhaps, encouraged into growing again.

Cixous (1992) talks about coming to writing. I remember a coming to writing and, like Jonathan, for me Jane was also always there; she always had something to do with it; there were always moments. And although I can never put a fix on a specific time, as Jonathan says here, "(there) was a moment when I understood that I could do this. I could write." I (too) could write. I resist the category of difference, writer, and I resist the category of difference, collaborative writer. I accept the differentiation that writing exists and in the always diffracting possibilities of these movements this (Deleuzian) sense of (always) becoming (collaborative) writer just about works for me. Something happened and keeps on happening in the "between the two" that we call becoming-Ken-Jonathan: it

---

[1] This was a phrase I enjoyed learning from Cindy Gowen, an American colleague and friend who was in the same doctoral program at the same time as Jonathan and me.

started in the middle back then and keeps creeping up behind our backs like a refreshing summer breeze and starting again: right here, right now, in the middle.

References:

Cixous, H. (1992). *"Coming to writing" and other essays* (D. Jenson, Ed.). Cambridge, MA: Harvard University Press.

Milton, J. (1960). *Paradise lost,* Book 9 (E. Tillyard, Ed.). London: George G. Harrap.

Woolf, V. (1985). *Moments of being,* 2nd ed. (Jeanne Schulkind, Ed.). London: Harcourt Brace.

Ken Gale

20th January 2015

It Is Good to Be Part of Something

Jonathan here tells how his participation in the seminars involves several elements of human life. It is not only seminars with a predetermined content area. His experience and the importance these seminars come to play in his life involve the routine of the drive there, overnight stays with friends, and mornings on the way to the university. It involves the joint employment with texts and the freedom to choose assignment topic, linking literature to personal interests. "It was good to be part of something," he writes. The participation is central, and the sense of belonging and the relationships are strengthened through joint activities, such as the discussions at the seminars and joint participation in conferences. This is indeed the experience of the non-divided "mind, body, activity and culturally organized settings," which includes others as mentioned by Lave (1988, p.1). The experiences are suspended in time and space and continue to take place "in the middle" as Ken notes at the end.

When we accept this form of time experience and this integration of a life lived and the life as a researcher, the question about work-life balance, or what we want to do after the PhD, becomes more complex. It is no longer simply a matter of making plans, or remembering to take time off, or about developing a timetable for when you are at the office and how to finish in the shortest time possible. Still, some kind of time management is crucial for the creation of a rewarding, effective, and enjoyable research life. There is always more to be done. It can always be better. It involves hard work and also a willingness to let go and move on. Living and thriving as a researcher thus involves knowing when it is time to stop. It involves the ability to speed up and slow down. This however does not only apply to finishing the dissertation. Finishing the dissertation should never be regarded as the ultimate goal. Rather, knowing when it is time to stop—to take a break or to move on the other tasks, is a crucial researcher competency throughout working life.

There Is Always Work To Do

There is a saying that there are only two kinds of dissertations: the perfect ones, and the ones that are finalized. The dissertation has to be submitted. So do conference abstracts, papers, revised papers, teaching material, and presentations throughout a research career. In the words of Van Maanen (1988/2011, p. 120): "We know that our analyses are not finished, only over." A friend of ours, a professor in education, aptly told her husband when he asked if she would like to join him for a movie or if she had work to do: "I always have work to do." This was not a complaint, nor was it a decision of joining him or not. It was just a fact. Whether we go for a movie or to our office, we have to decide for ourselves. There is no right or wrong. As Becker reminded us in Chapter 7, we may work hard but accomplish little.

Watching a movie does not make a paper. However, going to the movies may be a good decision if you do not actually get any work done. Becker points to the self-imposed suffering that stems from the idea that we must at least not *enjoy* doing something else when we feel we ought to be working.

Becker on Hard Work

Equating time spent and quality may in fact be empirically false. Painting teachers encourage students not to over paint a picture, continuing to put paint on the canvas until an initially good idea is buried in a muddy mess. Writers can worry a piece to death, fussing over adjectives and word order until readers respond to the effort that went into the polishing more than to the thought the prose was supposed to convey. More work may not produce a better product. On the contrary, the more we think about it, the more we may introduce irrelevant considerations and inappropriate qualifications, insist on making connections that needn't be made—until we bury the thought in Byzantine ornamentation. "More is better" is no more true than "less it better." Yes, writing needs reworking and thought. But how much? The answer should be sought pragmatically, not in fixed attitude. (Becker, 1986/2007, pp. 131–132)

We may even feel less guilty if we drag time, unproductively, in front of the PC or if we are caught up in distractions at the office.

Also, universities might not always be the best and most stimulating places to do the writing or to get things done—there may be other more creative places to write your dissertation, even if this is not the kind of message most university administrators would like to hear. In Mihaly Csikszentmihalyi's book *Creativity, Flow and the Psychology of Discovery and Invention,* we learn more about this through an interview with a professor of philosophy. The professor warns young people who wish to study philosophy at university that university is no longer a place where it is possible to be creative. To have the necessary peace and quiet for working, even the professor himself spends as little time as possible in his office because there he is constantly interrupted and never has the chance to flow. The point here is not to avoid social interaction and dialogues with students and colleagues. Rather, it is a matter of experiencing and learning to seek out the right company, time, and place for different research tasks. If the work does not flow, it is much more tempting to procrastinate. Yet, if we can only tell efficient time from idle time retrospectively, as suggested in Chapter 4, we can experiment with productive procrastination strategies. The trick is to look for ways of working that involve more joy—if the present way of working is not productive. It might involve a temporary letting go of goals and taking some time to do something else, such as reading fiction, going to the movies, or going for a run. It may also involve experimenting with different places to work. Remember that Hemingway produced some of his best work at Parisian cafes.

Always Heading Somewhere

Most PhD students put a lot of hard work and a good deal of life expectations into the doctoral journey. The doctorate is a rite of passage for most students and a pathway to new beginnings and opportunities. Some books about how to get things done and finish the dissertation underline that few doctoral students take responsibility for the dissertation and instead expect others to help them realize their goals and plans. The following quote comes to mind:

> Be aware of the journey and plan ahead: "You wouldn't go on a long journey without plotting your route ahead of time or programming your GPS, Also, while driving you would begin to look for the next gas station once you noticed your tank was below a quarter full. In a similar fashion, as a doctoral student you are responsible for your own path through the university, the defence of your proposal, your research, and then your final defence. Too many of my students put the responsibility on the university and never look ahead; this only slows them down and frustrates them." (James & Slater, 2014, p. xxiii).

While we agree that a GPS, or some kind of plan, and taking responsibility for the kind of stance and identity you wish to pursue throughout is important, we would also argue that the need for collaboration is central. The GPS, or the plan, is not merely an individual responsibility. The ability to put your plan to use has much to do with the resources available in your research community, including pathways that might be mapped out for students to follow, feedback opportunities, and much more. And while the GPS shows specific goals in mind, as we learned in Chapter 7, those are often formed after action as a kind of "retrospective explanation for what people think they must have been doing" (Gioia, 2006, pp. 1713–1714). Certainly, we are always heading somewhere and it is good to attempt to reflect on the obstacles we encounter, and try and make the most of them, making relevant decisions along the way. In the end, this will help to make the trip easier and result in a more fruitful learning experience.

"Let's Start Before We're Ready"

As we have discussed, there is nothing wrong with goal setting and planning per se. But the act of setting your goals is never enough and should never just aim at finishing the dissertation. A publication plan, for example, can be valuable in the creation of a desired career beyond the "Dr." title (see Thomson & Kamler, 2012). The problems arise if this strenuous "GPS strategy" prevents us from paying attention to and relying on the kinds of inspirations that occur unexpectedly.

At the 2015 Berlinale press conference for Terrence Malick's movie *Knight of Cups*, the lead male actor, Christian Bale, commented on how the mantra throughout the film was "Let's start before we are ready." One of the producers, Sarah Green, explained that working with Malick for more than a decade has taught her to be light on her feet: "All the planning and organization that one might normally do, does not actually serve his style. We look like a student film: a couple of vans and people running around. So we are very much in the moment, aiming to capture what might happen. It takes a lot of trust, and looseness, and openness." Natalie Portman, the lead actress, said that working with Malick reminded her that the rules and rituals of filmmaking are not compulsory: "You have to find your own way, and to allow the mistakes, and welcome the problems," she said. "What others might consider a problem, Terry will approach as an opportunity." If it starts raining, Malick will shoot in the rain, rather than change the schedule, Portman said, commenting that "every day is a search for something beautiful . . . it is a great way to go" (Barraclough, 2015 and several other media between February 5 and 15, 2015).

Abandoning the Rules

What these comments do not address, however, are all those rules every filmmaker must obey—technology, communication, financial, production, and advertising issues. The point is not that there are no rules; rather, the point is that opportunities might arise from temporarily abandoning the rules in order to see what might happen. This is obviously a strategy that applies to art practices such as filmmaking; yet, as researchers we can, much in the same way, question the rules and invite mistakes and imperfection into our work and life. It is often said that we *acquire* knowledge, *gain* insight, and *make* new discoveries. Rarely do we hear of scientific work being understood in terms of *dropping something, letting go,* or *getting lost.* Lather's (2007) "methodology of getting lost" in the landscape of knowledge or the landscape of science can, though seemingly contradictory, be helpful in this regard. Lather (2007, p. 136) argues that we should cultivate the ability to engage with "not knowing" and to move toward a "vacillation of knowing and not knowing." Wandering and getting lost become methodological practices.

Unpleasant Confusion

Most of the time, research seems to be occupied with "seeking out" a destination, making the "right" decisions, and "finding" answers. Based on Pitt and Britzman (2003), Lather calls insights attained through struggle "difficult knowledge" (Lather, 2007, p. 13). While "lovely knowledge" reinforces what we think we want, a "difficult knowledge" allows the feelings of lostness to become the very force of the research practice. Confusion can force us to act and think *differently* about what we are looking at, and what we wish to learn. Doctoral students invariably begin their work expecting to see certain events occur and may construct their research journeys around those expectations. However, if we too eagerly head for pre-designed destinations, that is, for lovely knowledge, we risk finding only what we intended to search for. By including unpleasant confusion, our research can become more sensitive to the complexity of the field and raise new questions (Wegener & Aakjær, in press). As researchers we may also inadvertently get lost and confused, but we can turn these experiences into a deliberate strategy. The trick is to avoid an instinct to regain control as quickly as possible. In Weick's words:

> When we are confused, we pay closer attention to what is happening in order
> to reduce the confusion. Later, all we remember is that this period of confusion
> was an unpleasant experience. What we often fail to realize is that we also

learned a lot of details while struggling with the confusion. Those struggles and their consequences comprise learning, even if momentarily they don't feel that way. (Weick, 2009, p. 20)

In this perspective, it is clear that we should not rush to the planned destination. This is not to suggest that we throw away the GPS. The point is that a gaze fixed at the GPS simply in order to find the supposedly fastest route results in a research style where we pay less attention to the landscape. Sometimes a fixed gaze at the GPS is necessary. We should not give in to every sudden impulse or walk down any beautiful path. Planning is necessary. Yet at times refraining from planning or abandoning a plan may be equally necessary. The GPS must be turned off to allow for the unpredictability of bodily and affective experiences and open-ended problems. This balancing act resembles the abduction process in research, in which researchers convert uncertainty into a novel (interim) certainty, which in turn generates new uncertainty. Self-consciously turning the GPS on and off (and curiously observing the effects) can thus be a metaphor for the dialectical movement between paying attention to the present and planning for the future.

Stepping Stones for a Future Career

This book is about to end. We hope it can serve as a stepping stone for the reader. The book is written to encourage many more students to enjoy the ride of the PhD journey and to get the most out of the obstacles met along the way. Before leaving the work to you, we will end with a story of apprenticeship and how this line of thinking about one's career can be liberating, because it relieves you of the burden of having to find your own style and be original. Furthermore, this story underlines how the role of mentors and gatekeepers cannot be underestimated when it comes to securing or exploring a future career in research. Even if apprenticeship can be accused of leading to reproductive learning, it is the basis for finding one's own style. The story goes as follows:

The Artist Andreas Golder

In 2011, Lene got the chance to interview Andreas Golder, a Russian-born artist who resides in Berlin and who has been hailed one of the greatest artists in 21st-century Germany. If you do not inhabit the art world, Andreas Golder may not exactly be a big name, but within the art world, he is widely regarded as a man who has renewed the art of painting. Golder was born in Yekaterinburg, Russia, in 1979 and moved to Germany after the fall of the Berlin Wall in 1989. He has exhibited his work in Denmark on numerous occasions and has also appeared at the world-renowned White Cube gallery in London. Golder is commonly described as an artist who combines his training in realistic and representative techniques with more abstract elements—the physical and the metaphysical. What is interesting here: How does he work his artistic process, and what aspects does he personally regard as key to his success?

"I Do Not Know If I'm an Artist"

Golder is surrounded by smoke and steam when we interview him. One cigarette after another is ending its existence among its fellows in a plastic cup, while we take in and discuss the paintings on the walls and the sculptures in the room. Golder explains that he never precisely planned on being an artist but that it was more a result of circumstances. He says that he is just as happy lying down in front of the TV as he is painting but that he feels ill when he is not working on a painting in one form or another. The first thing Golder emphasizes in the interview is that he is uncertain whether he is truly an artist:

> It's the same every time people ask me, "How did you become an artist? When did you decide?" And each time, I'm just totally confused. How should I know whether I'm an artist at all? That's up to people to figure out when I'm no longer around. I just do what I do. Yesterday, I saw a good movie, *The Dark Knight*. There's a scene where the Joker says, "I'm chaos. I'm just a mad dog chasing after cars, and when I catch one, I don't know what I'm supposed to do with it." That's how I am when I paint.

Have you ever felt the same, the difficulties involved in answering how you became a researcher? As described by Golder, one relevant answer to the question might be to let others decide, or at least to pay attention to the importance of the audience in judging if you are on the right track. During the interview, we ask how Golder learned what he does, and he underlines how no specific method got him going: "It just came to me. In fact, there was no one who told me how I should do it, or what I should do. I think you need to find your own way. And there really isn't one correct method you can learn. It's quite individual."

> I went to art school in Russia and Berlin. In Russia, when I was a child—they have these special schools for athletes, ballerinas, and so on. They still do. I was just

there two weeks ago, at my old school. But now it's a very privileged school, only for the rich children. It was strange for me to see. In the old days, anyone could go there, but now it's about money, and it's horrible because a lot of children don't have the money, right? But yeah, they taught me all of the realistic techniques, and it was a very academic education. I could already paint as a nine-year-old. But you probably know this famous line from Picasso: "I could paint like Raphael when I was nine years old, but it took me another 30 years to learn how to paint a picture." [Andreas laughs.] I think it's the same for me.

The Craft of Finding One's Own Style

One thing is being able to paint; it is something else entirely to be able to paint pictures. Mastery of the technique is, Golder stresses, not enough. Making paintings involves entering a social practice—a sort of chain of other artists between whom one must make oneself a place and find oneself a style. How one gets there is difficult to say. Golder nevertheless reveals a bit of his "method" in our interview. Maybe it is an advantage to have access to a privileged school in which you learn to master the basic principles. And maybe this element of craft lies at the core of the quest for creativity, while the quest also requires that a person find his or her own style.

> Yeah, it all takes a long time. Learning the technique is pretty simple. It's almost a sort of copying practice. But I mean Renaissance artists and the great figurative painters became masters because they did more than just translate tradition. They added something to it. As a child, I also copied intensively. All of the old masters. It was part of our education. So when you talk about creativity, it's actually about stealing. Someone has done it before; you take it and continue. I mean, in the old days, we didn't even talk about artists but about masters and apprentices. Apprentices just continued their masters' lines, and that's why I'm so interested in the old masters. What's laughable is that there are so many young artists today who want to create something new all the time, and it's just "me, me, me." They just want to create something new without having any goal. And that's why all that "creativity" stuff has just a bit too much of a "housewife" whiff to it. They sit there and want to create something totally new. But it's more about doing something good and honestly. That's what I think.

Golder thus prefers the old apprenticeship tradition in which the apprentice, nearly by definition, is tasked with continuing the line that the master has already begun. He also feels that apprenticeship represents a correction to today's intolerable self-absorption. What we might learn from Golder's story is that finding one's own style and moving from being a doctoral student to becoming a complete researcher is really a matter of continuing a tradition and letting go of the quest for originality.

Good Advice for the PhD Student

- Keep challenging the premise that it hurts.
- Accept that, occasionally, it does hurt.
- Embrace confusion and uncertainty; and seek out ways to mine these feelings for research gold—keep a "confusion diary," get an "uncertainty pen pal," or invite people you like to a "getting lost study group."
- Give up the quest for originality and trust that your process of handling the material (theory, data, and academic writing conventions) with curiosity and persistence will produce worthwhile research output.
- Now and then, read page 176 in Howard Becker's *Writing for Social Scientists*: "Understand that the troubles you may have are not entirely your own doing, not the result of some terrible personal defect, but something build into the organization of academic life" (Becker, 1986/2007).
- Scan the research landscape for participation opportunities, and try out different relations and collaborations both inside and outside your institution and field of research. A diversity of involvement makes it easier to select and, just as crucial, to deselect people and activities that make you feel bad, sad, or bored. Set your GPS on destination "Encouragement."

Good Advice for the Supervisor

- Encourage the student to seek out both lovely and difficult knowledge. Embrace uncertainty together.
- Discuss with your student possible career trajectories, and together seek out work tasks and research outlets (conferences, journals) that support a desired trajectory beyond the dissertation work.
- If you want to keep the student in the research community, invite the student to be involved in your research endeavors, such as coauthorship, shared conference participation, or funding applications.
- If the student does not thrive, go into dialogue beyond goal-setting strategies. Do not accept the frequently used solution put forward by exhausted doctoral students that "I just need to pull myself together." If this was the solution, it would have been executed.
- Repeated dissatisfaction with the dissertation process may be addressed in terms of seeking out trajectories other than those the student anticipated. Dialogues about different career paths may be needed.
- Introduce the student to other masters.
- Ask the student to take responsibilities as a master for newcomers.

Conclusion

Living a life as a researcher is a never-ending iterative process of becoming. It is processes extended in time and space, involving not only the acquisition of knowledge and skill but identity formation and a sense of professional self in the landscape of professional practices and resources available. The professional life as a researcher involves identity formation that is never fully accomplished, always in a process of learning and participation. Accordingly, the master, though an expert in her field, is not at the end point of a linear professional process, to which the student can or should solely direct her gaze or plan to head for. There are no endpoints. The dissertation is not an endpoint and neither is the title of Professor. Researchers, as most other professionals, must continually adapt to new knowledge and changing social practices; that is, learning and identity formation is a lifelong journey. Closure and putting an end to uncertainty are not reachable or desirable goals of this journey.

Sometimes, pushing the gas pedal to the metal on the highway makes you travel the journey. At other times, it can be a laborious walk. Many minor roads, that is, fringe thoughts and hunches, must be abandoned in order to move forward. Yet, what we have advocated are, now and then, to abandon planning and be light on one's feet. When we move slowly, maybe get lost, and take our time to notice the landscape we are traveling, we will discover an abundance of resources available to make the journey enjoyable and rewarding.

References

Barraclough, L. (2015, February 8). Berlin: Christian Bale and Natalie Portman on working with Terrence Malick. *Variety,* the web magazine. Retrieved from http://variety.com/2015/film/global/berlin-christian-bale-and-natalie-portman-on-working-with-terrence-malick-1201427925/.

Becker, H. S. (1986/2007). *Writing for social scientists: How to start and finish your thesis, book, or article* (2nd ed.). London: University of Chicago Press.

Brinkmann, S. (2008), *Identitet: udfordringer i forbrugersamfundet* [Identity: Challenges of consumer society]. Århus: Klim.

Dreier, O. (2008). Learning in structures of social practice. In: S. Brinkmann, C. Elmholt, G. Kraft, P. Musaeus, K. Nielsen, & L. Tanggaard (Eds.), *A qualitative stance: Essays in honor of Steinar Kvale* (pp. 85–96). Aarhus: Aarhus University Press.

Gale, K., Speedy, J., & Wyatt, J. (2010). Gatecrashing the oasis? A joint doctoral dissertation play. *Qualitative Inquiry, 16*(1), 21–28.

Gioia, D. A. (2006). On Weick: An appreciation. *Organization Studies, 27*(11), 1709.

Greeno, J., & The Middle School Mathematics Through Applications Project Group. (1998). The situativity of knowing, learning, and research. *American Psychologist, 53*, 5–26.

Holzkamp, K. (1998). Daglig livsførelse som subjektvidenskabeligt grundkoncept. *Nordiske Udkast 2*, 3–31.

James, E. A., & Slater, T. (2014). *Doctoral book review: Writing your doctoral dissertation or thesis faster: A proven map to success.* Thousand Oaks, CA: Sage.

Kirshner, D., & Whitson, J. A. (1997). Editors' introduction. In D. Kirshner & J. A. Whitson (Eds.), *Situated cognition: Social, semiotic, and psychological perspectives* (1–16). Mahwah, NJ: Lawrence Erlbaum Associates.

Kundera, M. (1999). *Immortality*: New York: Harper Collins.

Kundera, M., & Asher, L. (1997). *Slowness: A Novel.* New York: Perennial.

Lather, P. A. (2007). *Getting lost: Feminist efforts toward a double(d) science.* New York: State University of New York.

Lave, J. (1988). *Cognition in practice: Mind, mathematics and culture in everyday life.* Cambridge: Cambridge University Press.

Lave, J. (2011). *Apprenticeship in critical ethnographic practice* (p. 3). Chicago and London: The University of Chicago Press.

Lave, J., & Wenger, E. (1991). *Situated learning: Legitimate peripheral participation.* Cambridge: Cambridge University Press.

MacIntyre, A. 1985. *After virtue: A study in moral theory* (2nd ed.). London: Duckworth.

Packer, M. J., & Goicoechea, J. (2000). Sociocultural and constructivist theories of learning: Ontology, not just epistemology. *Educational Psychologist, 35*(4), 227–241.

Pitt, A., & Britzman, D. (2003). Speculations on qualities of difficult knowledge in teaching and learning: An experiment in psychoanalytic research. *Qualitative Studies in Education, 16*(6), 755–776.

Thomson, P., & Kamler, B. (2012). *Writing for peer reviewed journals: Strategies for getting published.* London: Routledge.

Van Maanen, J. (1988/2011). *Tales of the field: On writing ethnography.* Chicago: University of Chicago Press.

Wegener, C., & Aakjær, M. K. (in press). Kicked out and let down: Breakdown-driven organizational research.

Wegener, C., Meier, N., & Ingerslev, K. (2014). Borrowing brainpower—sharing insecurities: Lessons learned from a doctoral peer writing group. *Studies in Higher Education*, ahead-of-print, 1–14.

Weick, K. E. (2009). *Making sense of the organization: Volume 2: The impermanent organization.* West Sussex: Wiley.

Index

Aalborg University, 67–68
Absorption, 61–63
Academic life, 140–142, 143–144
  See also Careers; Research
Acker, S., 33
Agee, J., xvii–xviii
Aitchison, C., 81, 82
Akre, V., 21
Alpert, F., 31
Alvesson, M., xvii
Amabile, T. M., 68
Amundsen, C., xv
Anxiety
  about future, 139–140
  performance, 85, 86, 100–101, 111
  in writing, xix, 78–79
Apprenticeship perspective
  in art, 152, 154–155
  benefits for creativity, 69
  developing voice, 41–42, 43
  distributed notion, 5, 77–78, 86, 90
  on feedback, 117–118
  learning style, 8, 9
  pedagogy, 10–12, 112
  pitfalls, 110
  research question development, 50–53
  in research training, xiii, xiv–xv,
    1–4, 5–7, 9–12, 31, 40
Apprenticeship writing, 78–79, 97, 111
  See also Coauthorship
Archimedes, 65–66
Artists, 152–155
Assessment
  formative, 119–120
  summarizing, 119–120
  See also Feedback

Atkinson, P., 20
Avery, H., 48–49

Badley, G., 80
Bager, Kenneth, 66
Bale, Christian, 150
Barab, S. A., 21
Barker, A., 70
Becher, T., xvi
Becker, H. S., 42, 47–48, 89, 124–125,
  126, 134–135, 148, 155
Billett, Stephen, 121–122, 133
Birk, Rasmus, 28–30
Bjørkvold, Jon-Roar, 45–46
Blind reviewers, 123–124
Boud, D., xviii, xix, 78, 81, 98
Boundary-crossing, 122
Bowker, Geoffrey, 44–45
Brinck, L., 20
Brinkmann, S., 4–5, 11, 25, 26–28, 70, 143
Brodin, E. M., 48–49
Brokering knowledge, 89
Brown, J. S., 3
Burns, R., 21
Byatt, A. S., 127

Calculability, 71
CAQDAS (computer-assisted qualitative
  data analysis software), 72
Careers
  publication plans, 150, 155
  stepping stones, 152
  transitions to, xxi, 38, 142–144,
    147–148
  work-life balance, 147–148
Cartier-Bresson, Henri, 68

Chen, S., xviii
Circularity of knowing, 130
Cixous, H., 146
Clark, A. D. M., xx–xxi, 116
Coauthorship
    advantages, xix, xx, 109–111
    advice on, 111
    after dissertation, 155
    common purpose, 108–109,
        110–111
    e-mails as data, xiii, 97–108
    feedback in, xx, 97, 108
    fine-tuning, 104–105
    focused asking for advice, 102–104
    idea testing, 100–101
    as pedagogic practice, xix–xx,
        96–97, 108–111, 112
    pitfalls, 110
    sharing completion, 105–106
    steep learning curve in, xix, 111
    theoretical framing, 101–102
Cochrane, R., 79–80
Cognitive apprenticeships, 3
    See also Apprenticeship perspective
Cognitive functionalism, 11, 14
Cognitive research, 13–14
Collaboration, xix, 15, 81, 112, 150
    See also Apprenticeship perspective;
        Coauthorship
Collins, A., 3
Communication. See E-mails
Complying and adjustment, 48–49
Computer-assisted qualitative data
        analysis software (CAQDAS), 72
Concentration, 61–62
Conferences, 132–134
Confusion, 151–152
    See also Uncertainty
Contractual style, 31
Control, 71–72
Co-writing. See Coauthorship
Craft
    apprenticeships, 69
    research as, 2, 4, 7, 10, 73
Creative breaks, 66–67
Creativity
    conditions for, 61–62, 65–67, 149
    encouraging, 49, 74
    incubating, 65–66, 67

mistakes and, 61
motivation and, 68
repeated routines and practices, 59,
    66–67
in research, 57–61, 69
tension with critical thinking, 48–49
time needed, 38–39
Critical thinking, 48–49
Csikszentmihalyi, Mihaly, 149
Cultures, of research communities, 6, 9,
    79, 85, 117, 134, 144
Curie, Marie, 61–62
Curie, Pierre, 61–62, 63, 67

Dance metaphor, 49–50
Deadlines, 61–62, 68
    See also Distractions
Defensive writing, 43–44, 126
Delamont, S., 4, 20
Devenish, R., xv, 81
Deviation, 59–61
Dewey, John, 49–50, 60
Directorial style, 31
Disclosure of chaos, 126–127
Dissertations. See Research questions;
        Writing
Distractions, 62–65, 66–67, 149
Distributed masters, 5, 77–78, 86, 90
Doctoral journey, 8–9, 142–144,
    149–152, 156
Doctoral programs
    activities, xix, 7, 10
    completion rates, xv
    dropout rates, xv
    goals, xix
    practices, 4
    resources, 14–15
    See also Matching; Research
        communities; Research training;
        Students; Supervision
Dreier, O., 141
Dreyfus, H., 9, 14
Dreyfus, S., 14
Dualism, 13–15
Duras, Marguerite, 64–65

Editors, 116, 127–130
Efficiency, 70–71
Elbow, P., 42, 43–44, 126

Elites, learning from, 5–6
Ellingson, L. L., 43, 126
Elmholdt, C., 12
E-mails as data, xiii, 97–108
Emotions, 14, 33
Engeström, Y., xvi, 11
Epistemological struggle, 88, 140
Everyday life research, 59, 87–89
Experimentation, 11–12, 43–44, 61, 82
Expertise, 82, 85
Expert–novice relationships. *See*
    Master–student relationships

Faculty members. *See* Supervisors
Failing, 30, 61
"Fast-food" mentality, 67–68
Feedback
    apprenticeship perspective on,
        117–118
    asking for, 127–129
    benefits, xx–xxi, 116
    in coauthorship, xx, 97, 108
    conflicting voices, 123
    formative assessment, 119–120
    giving, 129–130, 134–135
    from reviewers, 105–107
    sources, 116, 117, 125–126,
        131–132
    supervisory, 116–123, 135–136
    in writing groups, 82–85
Files, 40, 41, 89
First-cut publisher, 109
Forced incubation, 66
Forced novelty, 38–39
Formative assessment, 119–120
Freud, Sigmund, 62, 63
Friday detours, 64–65

Gale, Ken, 128, 144–147
Gap-spotting strategy, xvii
Gardner, Howard, 62
Gatfield, T., 31
Gioia, D. A., 38, 130
Glaveanu, Vlad, 131–132
Goicoechea, J., 141
Golde, C. M., xix, 112
Golder, Andreas, 69, 152–155
Gonsalves, A., 81
Graduate schools. *See* Doctoral programs

Graduate students. *See* Students
Graham, A., 33
Grant, B., 33
Green, Sarah, 150
Group pedagogies, xix, 81–82
    See also Peer groups
Grundfest, Harry, 88

Habits, 49–50, 60
Hargadon, A. B., 89–90
Hasrati, M., 10, 31
Hauge, Hans, 23–24
Health research, bodies in, 43
Holzkamp, K., 142
Horizontal learning, xviii, 86, 123
Hutchins, E., 8

Identities
    in peer learning, 82
    researcher, 7, 9, 141, 143–144, 156
    as self-interpretation, 143
    writing and, 79–80, 84–85, 111,
        145–147
Imagination, 59–60, 61, 69
    See also Creativity
Incubation, 65–66, 67
Individuality, 39
Inspiration, sources of, xvii–xviii, 40,
    59–60, 87–90
Isaksen, S. G., 22–23

Janesick, V. J., 49–50
Jazvac-Martek, M., xviii, 81
John-Steiner, Vera, 38–39, 61–62,
    67, 68

Kamler, B., xix, 5, 9, 41, 80, 97, 110
Kandel, Eric R., 87–88
Kant, Immanuel, 13
Kirsch, G. E., 88
Kirshner, D., 144
Klein, H. J., xx–xxi, 116
Klougart, Josefine, 64–65
Knausgaard, Karl Ove, 116, 123–124
Knowledge
    brokering, 89
    coproduction, xv
    difficult, 151
Kroll, J., 39–40

Kundera, Milan, 142–143
Kvale, S., 2, 3, 10, 14, 24–25, 27, 46–47

Laissez-faire style, 31
Lamm, R., 21
Landscape metaphor, xiii–xiv, xvi, 2,
    8–9, 11–12, 15, 40–41, 151
Language, pretentious, 46–48
    See also Writing
Lassig, C. J., 85
Lather, P. A., 151
Lave, J., xvi, 3, 10, 11, 117, 147
Learning
    contexts, xvi, 11
    by failing, 61
    by giving feedback, 134–135
    horizontal, xviii, 86, 123
    identity formation and, 144
    practice, xiv, 2
    processes and contexts, 21–22
    purpose, 141
    quick, 67–68
    reciprocal trust, 23–24
    separation from subject matter, 13–14
    situated, 11, 141
Lee, A., xviii, xix, 78, 81, 82
Lee, S., 10
Leth, Jørgen, 66, 69
Lewis, R., 21
Life of Brian, 39
Literature reviews, 41, 83–84
Lockheart, J., 81
Løgstrup, K. E., 23
Lovitts, B. E., 58
Ludvigsen, S., 21

MacIntyre, Alasdair, 143
Malfroy, J., 81
Malick, Terrence, 150
Master–student relationships, 5–7, 10
    See also Apprenticeship perspective
Matching
    challenges, 33–34
    criteria, xvii, 26, 34
    ideal fits, xvi–xvii
    importance, 24–26
    mismatches, 20, 28–30, 31–33
    successful, 20, 22–23, 24–25, 26–28
McAlpine, L., xv, xviii, 81

McDonaldization of research, 69–73
McMorland, J., 97–98
Meier, Ninna, 31–33, 43–46, 83–85, 140
Mentors, xiv, 3, 22–23, 33
    See also Apprenticeship perspective
Meta-analysis, 117
Methods. See Research methods
Mills, C. W., 3, 4, 40, 41, 73, 89, 90
Milton, John, 146
Mjelde, L., 12
Mottelson, Ben, 72
Mozart, Wolfgang Amadeus, 68
Murakami, Haruki, 57–58
Mutuality, 82, 84, 85

Nancarrow, C., 70, 72
Negotiated order model, 20–21, 33
Networks, xiv, xviii–xix, 62, 81, 91,
    133, 134
    See also Peer groups
Newman, S. E., 3
Nielsen, K., 8, 118–119
Nietzsche, Friedrich, 14
Nobel Prizes, 5–6, 62, 72, 87–88
Noe, R. A., xx–xxi, 116
Noller, Ruth B., 22–23
Novelty. See Originality

Obstacles, as challenges, xviii, 58
Occupied territory metaphor, 40–41, 48
Originality and contribution, xvii–xviii,
    37–39, 46, 47, 48–49, 54–55, 90
    See also Research questions
Orlikowski, W. J., 98

Packer, M. J., 141
Paré, A., 116–117, 135
Parry, O., 20
Pastoral style, 31
Paulson, J., 81
Pedagogy
    coauthorship as practice, xix–xx,
        96–97, 108–111, 112
    of doing, 11–12, 108–109, 117–119
    group, xix, 81–82
    relational, xv
    research on, 13–14
    See also Apprenticeship perspective;
        Learning

Peer groups
  feedback from, 131–132
  importance, xviii–xix
  nonproductive interactions, 86
  participation in, xix, 142
  writing groups, xviii, 43, 81–87
Peer learning, 81
Peer-review culture, 79, 85–86, 134
Performance anxiety, 85, 86,
    100–101, 111
PhD programs. *See* Doctoral programs
Picasso, Pablo, 48, 154
Pillutla, M. M., 38
Plato, 13
Plucker, J. A., 21
Portman, Natalie, 150
Power relations, xiii, 5, 33, 110–111
Practice learning, xiv, 2
Predictability, 71
Pretentious language, 46–48
Procrastination, 149
  See also Distractions
Publishing
  plans, 150, 155
  pressures, 123–124
  See also Coauthorship; Writing

Qualitative research
  methods, 70–71, 72
  projects, 28–30
  skills development, 49–50
  software, 72
  standardization, 69–70, 72
  See also Research
Quick learning, 67–68

Reading groups, 131, 142
Reciprocal trust, 23–24
Research
  abandoning rules, 151
  as craft, 2, 4, 7, 10, 73
  as creative endeavor, 57–61, 69
  as doing, xvi, 2, 4–5, 7, 10–12
  embodied and materialized practice,
    4, 10–11
  as knowing, xvi, 2, 7, 10–12
  landscape metaphor, xiii–xiv, xvi, 2,
    8–9, 11–12, 15, 40–41, 151
  McDonaldization, 69–73

  as social practice, 11–12
  See also Qualitative research
Research communities
  access to, 9
  belonging to, 9, 28, 144
  collaboration, 15, 81, 112, 150
  cultures, 6, 9, 79, 85, 117, 134, 144
  international, 106–107
  invitations, 98–100, 106–107, 155
  learning opportunities, xviii, 10
  resources, 150
  See also Doctoral programs;
    Matching
Researchers
  careers, 38, 142–144, 147–148, 150,
    152, 155
  identities, 7, 9, 141, 143–144, 156
  lives, 140–142, 143–144,
    148–149, 156
Researcher voice, 41–42, 43–46
  See also Writing
Research methods, 3, 39–40, 70–71, 72
Research projects
  deadlines, 61–62, 68
  fieldwork, 70–71
  funding, 70, 72
  impact, 37–39, 54–55
  sense-making, 52
Research questions
  advice on, 54
  evolution, xvii, 50–53
  gap-spotting strategy, xvii
  keeping the ball rolling, 90–91
  organizing ideas, 40, 41
  originality and contribution,
    xvii–xviii, 37–39, 46, 47,
    48–49, 54–55, 90
  sources of inspiration, xvii–xviii, 40,
    59–60, 87–90
  sub-questions, xvii
Research talent, 20, 21–22
Research training
  career preparation, xxi, 38,
    142–144, 147–148
  conflicts with real life, 142
  defining moments, 26–27
  finishing on time, xv, 30–33, 140
  as journey, 8–9, 142–143
  personal narratives, xiv, 4

stewardship, 112
stretching metaphor, 49–50
See also Apprenticeship perspective;
Doctoral programs; Supervision
Richardson, L., 80, 126
Ritzer, G., 70, 71–72
Rohan, L., 88
Roth, W.-M., 10
Rules, abandoning, 151

Sandberg, J., xvii
Sawyer, K. R., 65–66
Scaffolding, 3, 31, 44
Sennett, R., 69
Situated learning, 11, 141
Skou, Jens, C., 72
Slowness, 142–143, 148
Socialization, 20–21, 96
Social media, 62, 66
Speedy, Jane, 125, 145, 146
Star, Susan L., 44–45
Starting before ready, 150
Stepping stones, 152
Sternberg, R. J., 58
Stretching, 49–50
Students
advice for, 15, 34, 54, 73, 91, 111,
135, 155
agency, 96, 112
experiences, xvii–xviii, 41, 79, 89,
142, 147
isolation, xviii, 81, 91
research talent, 20, 21–22
responsibilities, 149–150
transitions to research careers, 38,
142–144, 147–148
See also Doctoral programs;
Matching; Peer groups;
Research training
Stumbling, 59–61
Summarizing assessment, 119–120
Supervision
as black box, 96
candidate-dependent, 121–123
dialogues, xix, 119
expectations, 26
negotiated order model, 20–21, 33
power relations, xiii, 5, 33, 110–111

as process and production, 95–96,
108–111, 118–119
reciprocal trust, 23–24
reflection on, 97–98
student agency in, 96, 112
styles, 31
technical rationality model, 20
See also Apprenticeship perspective;
Coauthorship; Feedback;
Research training
Supervisors
ability to transfer expertise, xiv
advice for, 15, 34, 54, 73, 91–92,
111, 135–136, 155
facilitator role, xix, 21, 99
as mentors, xiv, 22–23, 33
roles, 31, 33, 39–40, 109, 121–122
skills and expertise, 31
See also Coauthorship; Feedback
Szulevicz, Thomas, 120–121

Talent. *See* Research talent
Tanggaard, Lene, 4–5, 8, 11, 24–25, 28,
98–108, 123, 152–153
Teaching, "fast-food" mentality,
67–68
See also Learning; Pedagogy
Thau, S., 38
Thomson, P., 5, 9, 41, 80, 110
Trajectories of participation, 144
Transactional functionality, 21
Trowler, P. R., xvi
Trust
reciprocal, 23–24
in writing groups, 82, 86

Uncertainty, 139–140, 155
See also Confusion

Van Maanen, J., 38, 49, 125–126, 148
Vibskov, Henrik, 61
Vir, J., 70
Voice, in writing, 41–42, 43–46,
64–65, 82
Vygotsky, L., 12

Wagner, J., 90, 135
Walker, G. E., xix, 10, 112

Wegener, Charlotte, 43–46, 50–53, 63–65, 82–85, 98–108, 126–129, 132, 133
Weick, K. E., 38, 130, 151–152
Wells, D. H., 66
Wenger, E., 10, 117
Whitson, J. A., 144
Wolcott, H. F., 97
Woolf, Virginia, 146
Work-life balance, 147–148
    See also Careers
Wright, T., 79–80
Writing
    advice books, 80, 140
    anxieties about, xix, 7
    apprenticeships, 78–79, 97, 111
    challenges, xix, 78–79, 149, 155
    conventions, 42–43
    as data collection, 80
    defensive, 43–44, 126
    dialogues, 43–46
    as discursive social practice, 96–97

feedback on, 116–117, 120–121, 123–125
finishing, 148–149
identity formation and, 79–80, 84–85, 111, 145–147
peer reviews, 79, 123–124
places, 148–149
pretentious language, 46–48
publication plans, 150, 155
reviewers of, 105–107, 123–124
rewriting, 86, 125
as social practice, 7–8
untidy texts, 125–127
voice in, 41–42, 43–46, 64–65, 82
    See also Coauthorship; Research questions
Writing classes, 97
Writing groups, xviii, 43, 81–87
Wyatt, Jonathan, 127–130, 144–147

Yates, J., 98

Zuckerman, H., 5–6